TRAILBLAZERS
in SCIENCE and TECHNOLOGY

The Leakey Family

UNEARTHING HUMAN ANCESTORS

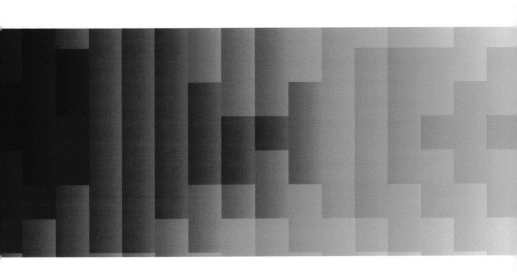

TRAILBLAZERS
IN SCIENCE AND TECHNOLOGY

The Leakey Family

UNEARTHING HUMAN ANCESTORS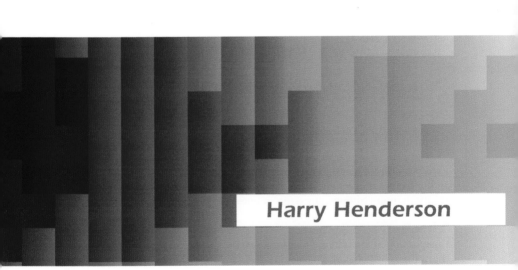

Harry Henderson

CHELSEA HOUSE
An Infobase Learning Company

The Leakey Family: Unearthing Human Ancestors

Chelsea House
An imprint of Infobase Learning
132 West 31st Street
New York NY 10001

Library of Congress Cataloging-in-Publication Data

Henderson, Harry.
   The Leakey family : unearthing human ancestors / Harry Henderson.
      p. cm. — (Trailblazers in science and technology)
   Includes bibliographical references and index.
   ISBN 978-1-60413-674-6
   1. Leakey, L. S. B. (Louis Seymour Bazett), 1903–1972. 2. Leakey, Mary D. (Mary Douglas), 1913–1996. 3. Leakey, Richard E. 4. Physical anthropologists—Tanzania—Olduvai Gorge—Biography. 5. Paleoanthropologists—Tanzania—Olduvai Gorge—Biography. 6. Fossil hominids—Tanzania—Olduvai Gorge. 7. Excavations (Archaeology)—Tanzania—Olduvai Gorge. 8. Olduvai Gorge (Tanzania)—Antiquities. I. Title. II. Series.
   GN50.6.L43H46 2011
   599.9092'2—dc22   2011001972

Text design by Erika K. Arroyo
Composition by Hermitage Publishing Service
Illustrations by Bobbi McCutcheon
Photo research by Suzanne M. Tibor
Cover printed by Yurchak Printing, Landisville, Pa.
Book printed and bound by Yurchak Printing, Landisville, Pa.
Date printed: June 2012
Printed in the United States of America

10 9 8 7 6 5 4 3 2 1

This book is printed on acid-free paper.

For those who spend countless painstaking hours unearthing
and piecing together the clues to our humanity . . .
What could be more human?

Contents

Preface

Trailblazers in Science and Technology is a multivolume set of biographies for young adults that profiles 10 individuals or small groups who were "trailblazers" in science—in other words, those who made discoveries that greatly broadened human knowledge and sometimes changed society or saved many lives. In addition to describing those discoveries and their effects, the books explore the qualities that made these people trailblazers, the personal relationships they formed, and way those relationships interacted with their scientific work.

What does it take to be a trailblazer, in science or any other field of human endeavor?

First, a trailblazer must have imagination: the power to envision a path where others see only expanses of jungle, desert, or swamp. Helen Taussig, Alfred Blalock, and Vivien Thomas imagined an operation that could help children whose condition everyone else thought was hopeless. Louis and Mary Leakey looked at shards of bone embedded in the rocks of an African valley and pictured in them the story of humanity's birth.

Imagination alone will not blaze a trail, however. A trailblazer must also have determination and courage, the will to keep on trudging and swinging a metaphorical machete long after others fall by the wayside. Pierre and Marie Curie stirred their witch's cauldron for day after day in a dirty shed, melting down tons of rock to extract a tiny sample of a strange new element. The women astronomers who assisted Edward Pickering patiently counted and compared white spots on thousands of photographs in order to map the universe.

Because their vision is so different from that of others, trailblazers often are not popular. They may find themselves isolated even from those who are working toward the same goals, as Rosalind Franklin did in her research on DNA. Other researchers may brand them as "outsiders" and therefore ignore their work, as mathematicians did at first with Edward Lorenz's writings on chaos theory because Lorenz's background was in meteorology (weather science), a quite different scientific discipline. Society may regard them as eccentric or worse, as happened to electricity pioneer Nikola Tesla and, to a lesser extent, genome analyst and entrepreneur Craig Venter. This separateness sometimes freed and sometimes hindered these individuals' creative paths.

On the other hand, the relationships that trailblazers do form often sustain them and enrich their work. In addition to supplying emotional and intellectual support, compatible partners of whatever type can build on one another's ideas to achieve insights that neither would have been likely to develop alone. Two married couples described in this set, the Curies and the Leakeys, not only helped each other in their scientific efforts but inspired some of their children to continue their path. Other partnerships, such as the one between Larry Page and Sergey Brin, the computer scientists-turned-entrepreneurs who founded the Internet giant Google, related strictly to business, but they were just as essential to the partners' success.

Even relationships that have an unhealthy side may prove to offer unexpected benefits. Pickering hired women such as Williamina Fleming to be his astronomical "computers" because he could pay them far less than he would have had to give men for the same work. Similarly, Alfred Blalock took advantage of Vivien Thomas's limited work choices as an African American to keep Thomas at his command in the surgical laboratory. At the same time, these instances of exploitation, so typical of the society of the times, gave the "exploited" opportunities that they would not otherwise have had. Thomas would not have contributed to lifesaving surgeries if he had remained a carpenter in Nashville, even though he might have earned more money than he did by working for Blalock. Fleming surely would never have discovered her talent for astronomy if Pickering had kept her as merely his "Scottish maid."

Competitors can form almost as close a relationship as cooperative partners, and like the irritating grain of sand in an oyster's shell that eventually yields a pearl, rivalries can inspire scientific trailblazers to heights of achievement that they might not have attained if they had worked unopposed. Tesla's competition with Thomas Edison to establish a grid of electrical power around U.S. cities stimulated as well as infuriated both men. Venter's announcement that he would produce a readout of humanity's genes sooner than the massive, government-funded Human Genome Project pushed him, as well as his rival, HGP leader Francis Collins, to greater efforts. The French virologist Luc Montagnier was spurred to refine and prove his suspicions about the virus he thought was linked to AIDS because he knew that Robert Gallo, a similar researcher in another country, was close to publishing the same conclusions.

It is our hope that the biographies in the Trailblazers in Science and Technology set will inspire young people not only to discover and nurture the trailblazer within themselves but also to trust their imagination, even when it shows them a path that others say cannot exist, yet at the same time hold it to strict standards of proof. We hope they will form supportive relationships with others who share their vision, yet will also be willing to learn from those they compete with or even dislike. Above all, we hope they will feel the curiosity about the natural world and the determination to unravel its secrets that all trailblazers share.

Acknowledgments

I would like to thank Frank K. Darmstadt for his help and suggestions, Suzie Tibor for her hard work in rounding up the photographs, and Bobbi McCutcheon for drawing the diagrams. And, as always, I would like to thank my wonderful wife, Lisa Yount, for all she has taught me about writing simply and clearly . . . and for so much more.

Introduction

Today, most of science seems to happen in well-equipped laboratories bristling with elaborate devices. Physicists have particle colliders and detectors. Biologists and medical researchers now have automatic DNA sequencers that can piece together genetic codes in minutes instead of years. Just about everyone has access to devices such as mass spectrographs for analysis of the chemical composition of a geological sample—or perhaps a bit of evidence from a murder investigation.

Even astronomers, who used to have to sit at the eyepiece of a giant telescope in a cold, drafty observatory, can now sit in a comfortable, air-conditioned office and view star fields or distant planets on a monitor screen. Indeed, the common factor in all modern science is the computer and the capabilities it brings to extract data and turn it into charts or pictures that are easy to visualize.

A SCIENCE THAT GETS ITS HANDS DIRTY

The search for clues to the origins of humanity has little in common with this sort of high-tech science. True, when bits of bone (or in rare cases, ancient DNA) find their way to the laboratory, the technicians and equipment there can determine with a considerable degree of accuracy when a creature lived, died, and was fossilized. For relatively "young" specimens, such as a Neanderthal who lived perhaps 35,000 years ago, the analysis of DNA is revealing their differences and similarities from modern humans and suggesting possibilities for the relationship between species.

However, there is no science without data. For paleoanthropologists such as the Leakey family (Louis, Mary, and Richard) featured in this volume in the Trailblazers in Science and Technology set, there are no machines for collecting or sorting the raw data. The data consists of fossils, artifacts, and other traces of creatures (including people rather like ourselves) who lived between tens of thousands and several million years ago.

The effort to unearth and understand evidence of early humanity takes a matter of years, even generations. When asked by interviewer Keith Bellows, "What quality do you admire most in your parents and grandparents?," Louise Leakey replied, "The sheer determination and perseverance that all of them have shown at different times when most of us might have given up." She points out that Louis and Mary Leakey did not find key fossils confirming their belief in the African origin of early humanity until 1959, after three decades of work.

Without access to some sort of electronic fossil detector, the paleoanthropologist is forced to depend on a pair of sharp, experienced human eyes and maybe a hunch (a good bit of luck does not hurt, either!). While the Hollywood archaeologist Indiana Jones seems to alternate his days between battling Nazis and ancient Templar knights and digging up treasure-filled tombs, unearthing fossil treasure requires a much more painstaking approach.

No one has ever found a complete million-year-old human skeleton resting gently in the ground. Typically, the first clues that something interesting might be underfoot might be a small shard of bone or a tooth. The shards might be a clue that some more substantial bones could be nearby, but water, erosion, or other geological forces may have scattered the original skeleton all along a hillside or ancient riverbed. As for the tooth or the protruding end of a bone, careful excavation with dental pick and brush might reveal a whole upper or lower jaw, or perhaps parts of a foot.

The working conditions in East Africa where the Leakeys toiled were also nothing like those of the laboratory scientist. There were poor or no roads (particularly in the earlier part of the 20th century). Vehicles did not have modern tires, let alone four-wheel drive, and breakdowns could be expected. Until the 1960s, there was no radio or other communications. All supplies had to be brought in, food tended to be limited in variety (sometimes supplemented by hunting), and finding enough drinking water was always a problem. On top of that there were potentially dangerous lions and unpredictable buffalo, as well as biting ticks and other nasty insects and a generous supply of pythons or poisonous adders.

Researchers such as Louis, Mary, and Richard Leakey and their modern counterparts have to be entrepreneurs and publicists to arouse public interest and attract private contributions to fund a season of fossil hunting. (In an interview by Christina Hernandez, Louise Leakey cites two challenges still faced by archaeological researchers in Africa: "distance" and "actually getting funding to do this work.") They then have to be project manager, safari organizer, camp boss, scout, and supervisor. Only then, after the specimens are safely in the museum or laboratory, can the science really begin.

It is probably not surprising that the kind of person who would persist in the search despite long odds and great hardships would often also come equipped with an oversized ego. The Leakeys and their rivals argued fiercely and even bitterly over many questions. A basic problem was determining how old a fossil really was, in a time before radioactive dating when only geological clues or a study of nearby animal fossils could be used to fix a relative date. Controversies over dating would bedevil the Leakeys, at one point almost destroying Louis's career.

The relationships between human species and their ancestors were (and are) another bone of contention. Louis believed that a line of species with essentially human characteristics could be traced back hundreds of thousands to millions of years. Others, such as Donald Johanson (discoverer of the famous Lucy), believe that a near-human family of species, the *australopithecines,* provided the main thrust toward humanity.

STORIES OF A FAMILY

The Leakey Family: Unearthing Human Ancestors, one volume in the Trailblazers in Science and Technology set, outlines what biographers have discovered about the Leakey family and explores their struggles, accomplishments, and failures. Chapter 1 introduces Louis Leakey and his remarkable childhood. Child of two white missionaries in Kenya, Louis grew up to be at least as much Kikuyu as British. Louis showed his independence by building his own house as a teenager. His explorations of the African countryside led to a fascination with ancient stone tools. Going to Cambridge University as a young man, Louis experienced considerable culture shock.

In chapter 2, Louis, having already undertaken a small expedition, begins his major fieldwork while seeking to establish the age of the earliest humans. He comes home in triumph, believing that he had vindicated his ideas.

Chapter 3 is a roller-coaster ride, both scientifically and emotionally. Louis, fresh from his first triumphs in the field, meets and falls in love with Mary Nicol, a talented artist with an interest in archaeology. The only problem is that Louis is already married. . . . When both his scientific evidence and his personal morals are challenged, it begins to look like a promising scientific career would come to an early end. On top of that, there is World War II and a new assignment for Louis: spy and police investigator.

In chapter 4, Louis, now joined by Mary, begins to rebuild his scientific reputation. Over a bit more than a decade, the couple goes on to make a series of key discoveries ranging from early ape ancestors to fossils that may represent the first steps on the road to humanity. (In between fossil hunting expeditions, Louis again becomes embroiled in intelligence work as a rigid white colonial establishment confronts Mau Mau militants.)

Chapter 5 finds the Leakey family enduring losses while a new career, that of Richard Leakey, is launched. As Louis and Richard both struggle with health problems, son and father begin to quarrel over the future of the Kenya National Museum.

In chapter 6, Louis is gone, but Richard is in his prime, battling Donald Johanson (discoverer of Lucy) over fossil dates and evolutionary relationships. Meanwhile Mary, continuing to work quietly in Laetoli, makes an astonishing discovery.

The conclusion looks at the Leakey legacy in *paleoanthropology,* expressed both in the anchoring of human origins in Africa and the development of techniques still used every day in the field by researchers such as Louise, daughter of Richard and Meave Leakey. These enduring legacies are contrasted with the promise and challenge of new techniques.

From Africa to Cambridge

Harry and Mary (May) Bazett Leakey were Christian missionaries in what was then called British East Africa (later Kenya). In 1901, Harry arrived in Africa first to prepare the way for his family. Their small mission was in a place called Kabete in the hills of central Kenya. From there one could see the great peaks of Mount Kenya and the famous Mount Kilimanjaro. Nearby was Nairobi. As the 20th century began, this future capital of Kenya was only a small town.

Even with all possible preparation, Mary's own journey to Kabete was difficult. In her earlier missionary service in coastal Kenya, she had become so ill that she was advised by doctors to abandon any thought of returning to Africa. Now she traveled from England with her children by steamship and the newly built railroad. When Harry met them in Nairobi he returned to the mission on horseback. Mary and the rest of the family, were carried on hammocks by pairs of men of the Kikuyu people, the main native group in the region.

As missionaries, the Leakeys were faced with a daunting task. There were few other missionaries in the area, and the people were desperately poor. Harry and Mary set about establishing schools and medical clinics. In turn, the people treated the Leakeys with affection and respect. Harry was given the nickname "Giteru," referring to his large beard. Mary became known as "Bibi," roughly meaning "Lady."

A LITTLE MIRACLE

Louis, the third child of Harry and Mary Leakey, was born on August 7, 1903, in a small house with a dirt floor and a leaky (no pun intended) thatched roof. His birth was premature, and given the primitive living conditions, Louis said in his early autobiography *White African,* his survival was "nothing short of a miracle."

When it became likely he would live, the child was placed in a wicker basket on the veranda of their house. Crowds of Kikuyu came to see little Louis—most had never seen a white infant before. Many people reached out and touched the baby, but another kind of gesture brought problems. Many Kikuyu tried to spit on the child—a traditional Kikuyu practice that assured they had not cursed him. Not surprisingly, Louis's mother tried to prevent this and kept a sponge nearby to wipe him. Later, in a *National Geographic* article, Melvin Payne would quote Louis as saying he had been the "best washed baby" in Kenya.

Harry's own health problems made a return to England necessary. He was suffering from dizziness, insomnia, ringing in the ears, and the prospect of a nervous breakdown. When the family returned to Kabete late in 1906, they were able to live in a somewhat more snug stone house. But now they found the countryside to be in some turmoil. The numbers of white settlers in the area were rapidly increasing, encouraged by a British program that offered cheap land to would-be farmers. The elevation of the area that became known as the White Highlands made for a cooler climate more hospitable to Europeans. The Kikuyu, however, were not consulted about the arrangements. The area where most of them lived was designated as a sort of reservation, but that did not stop parcels of it from being sold when needed by white settlers.

Such policies planted seeds for future unrest and conflict, but the world looked different from the point of view of little Louis. While adults tend to observe social boundaries, children seem to be more inclined to make friends where they find them. Young Louis and his younger brother Douglas and older sisters Gladys and Julia had a rather free, easygoing life. They did not go to school. (There was nothing considered suitable for white children.) They had a tutor who taught them in the morning. Afternoons were free for exploring nature. In an interview with biographer Virginia Morrell quoted in *Ancestral Passions,* Julia recalls that

> I was always Louis's friend, or should I say buddy, because we both preferred to look at everything from the natural history point of view and

collected every sort of animal and insect and bird. We skinned dead birds, made traps, and collected information. Louis in particular soon made friends with Kikuyu children his own age. They would shoot little bows and arrows, and play a game where one child would roll a hoop while another tried to throw a spear through it. Louis learned the Kikuyu language and spoke it at least as fluently as English.

THE WHITE KIKUYU

In 1911, the family made another return to Reading, England, taking the usual one-year furlough for missionaries plus an additional year to help Mary recover her health. Louis, now eight, found himself in school for the first time—a proper British school. As he would say in his autobiography *White African,* school made him feel "like a fish out of water." His stay at the school was brief. Harry used the time to set up a little preparatory school for Louis and three other boys. This was much more comfortable for Louis, though he still greatly missed the walks in the African forest with his Kikuyu friends.

When the family returned to Africa in 1913, they took along a Miss B. A. Bull, a tutor who was trained in the classics (ancient literature and languages such as Latin). Miss Bull found that she could not hold the interest of Louis very long. As far as he was concerned, the best part of the day was after tea-time, when they could go on nature walks. While Louis had little interest in Latin, he did like to collect flowers and other specimens from the countryside. One day, he watched in fascination while a chameleon and a tree snake engaged in a life-and-death struggle.

A HUT OF HIS OWN

As part of their journey toward adulthood, Kikuyu boys built their own huts and lived in them for several years, separated from their parents. Around this time, Louis asked his parents if he could live in a hut of his own like his Kikuyu friends. At first they were a bit doubtful about the idea, so Louis built three huts, each larger and more elaborate than the last. When they saw his energy and skill as a builder, they finally allowed the 14-year-old to live in a hut—or perhaps one might call it a small house.

Louis had continued to collect specimens from nature—birds' eggs, skins, nests, skulls, and stones. In *White African,* Louis later said that this hut represented freedom to him—a place that was exclusively his own, with everything in it chosen by himself.

Louis Leakey's early experiences with tribal life matured into a very useful ability to gain the support of native peoples for his expeditions. Here, he talks with Masai elders at Olduvai Gorge, Tanzania. (*Joe Scherschel/National Geographic/Getty Images*)

Louis also learned the patient hunting skills of the Kikuyu. In his book *Animals of East Africa*, Louis recalls that:

> . . . from Joshua [his close Kikuyu friend] I learned to camouflage my human form with leaves and small branches; to approach a quarry diagonally, and very alertly, and above all, never to show my arms.

Besides sneaking up on animals, Louis learned traditional Kikuyu games. In turn, he taught the Kikuyu boys (who were barefoot) how to play soccer.

As a mark of how well he was accepted by the Kikuyu, Louis underwent the secret rite of initiation to become a member of the tribe. No wonder that, as he notes in *White African*, Louis even dreamed in Kikuyu!

WAY OF THE HUNTER

Louis's experience of nature and the Kikuyu way of life would have a profound effect on his later career. Writing in a book for *National Geographic*, Louis explained that in his hunting experience:

. . . most important, I learned patience, for it was necessary to get quite close to an animal if it was to be killed with . . . short-range weapons—the bow and arrow, thrusting spear, or club. . . . . I have used much of what I have learned when trying to interpret the possible ways Stone Age man hunted and trapped his prey.

While *fossil* hunting is different from pursuing living animals, it requires similar patience and equally keen observation of one's surroundings. Perhaps just as important, living as a Kikuyu meant Louis could experience the world the way native Africans did. Understanding this point of view would help him later in wartime intelligence work and in trying to make the British authorities understand why so many of their colonial policies were failing.

WARTIME DISRUPTION

Because the African colonies generally lacked advanced schools, colonists and missionaries normally sent their children (boys at least) back to England when they were about 13. However, as Louis approached that age in 1914, World War I broke out. Great Britain and its colonies, together with allies such as France, Russia, and Japan, squared off against Germany, Austria-Hungary, Turkey, and Bulgaria. With German U-boats (submarines) attacking shipping, a trip back to England would be too risky.

Since both Britain and Germany had colonies in Africa, there was fear that the war would spread to that continent. The colonists in British East Africa prepared to defend the colony against a possible invasion from German East Africa (now Tanzania). The missionaries organized a Volunteer Carrier Corps of Kikuyu to help supply the British forces.

The Germans hoped to draw British forces away from Europe by threatening the African colonies. However the British were able to bring up reinforcements from their major colony in South Africa as well as from India, and the German efforts were unsuccessful. While the Volunteer Carrier Corps was not directly involved in the fighting, the Spanish influenza, a global pandemic, rapidly spread through the Kikuyu ranks and back to their homeland, effectively wiping out many Kikuyu villages. Many survivors felt that their people had been badly used as pawns in a conflict between white nations. At the same time, their experience showed the Kikuyu the power of organization—something that might gradually be turned toward a fight for independence.

TOOLS AND TRACES

Just as Louis was immersing himself in Kikuyu life, a new influence arrived from abroad. As a Christmas gift, a British cousin sent him a book called *Before History,* by R. H. Hall. While the Kikuyu had helped him become intimately acquainted with the vast expanse of space that was Africa, this book introduced Louis to the expanse of time over which human culture had developed. Just as many modern children become fascinated with dinosaurs that lived tens of millions of years ago, Louis was fascinated by the tens of thousands of years over which humans explored, hunted, and created families . . . leaving no written traces behind.

Nothing written, perhaps, but there was one thing—stone *tools.* At the time, most such tools had been found in Europe. They were made of *flint* and could be flaked into sharp pieces for cutting. (Flints could also be struck to make sparks to start a fire. Later they were used in flintlocks to ignite gunpowder in early firearms.)

Hall's book described how prehistoric people made and used flint tools. Fascinated, Louis began to look around the African landscape for such tools. He did not know that there was no flint anywhere in East Africa. However he did find a different form of stone—*obsidian.* Obsidian is a glassy-looking black stone—in fact, it is volcanic glass. Blades flaked from obsidian are extremely sharp. Today, they are used to make surgical scalpels sharper than the finest steel blades.

Louis began to collect pieces of obsidian that looked very much like the flint tool blades illustrated in Hall's book. When he showed them to his parents, they told him that they probably were not real tools. After all, they were not made of flint!

Meanwhile when Louis showed the obsidian pieces to his Kikuyu friends, they told him he was quite mistaken. Kikuyu did not have tools like that. No, these were razors used by the sky spirits, showered on the earth when they were too dull for further use. In *White African,* Louis remarked that the Kikuyu explanation had a certain logic to it:

> Most of the prehistoric obsidian implements and flakes in the Kikuyu country are buried fairly deeply in the soil . . . After a very heavy fall of rain, pieces of obsidian are perfectly noticeable, so it is not surprising that the Kikuyu think that they have come down out of the sky with the rain.

Finally, Louis took some of the obsidian objects to the Nairobi Museum, where he had become good friends with curator Arthur Loveridge. As he recounted in *White African*, Louis "thought he might laugh at me." However, Loveridge carefully examined Louis's finds and pronounced that some were "certainly implements." He also showed Louis obsidian arrowheads from the

TOOL OR NOT?

What image comes to mind when one hears the word "tool"? Probably a hammer, a screwdriver, or something similar. There is certainly no problem identifying these manufactured metal or wood objects as tools.

It is quite different with the first tools that humans made. Indeed, humans were not the first toolmakers. At its most basic, a tool can be defined as an object that is used to manipulate the environment or other objects in some useful way. Chimpanzees and even some birds can use sticks to extract termites or other insects for food. If the definition of tool is narrowed a bit to require that the object be prepared or fashioned in some way, one can still observe that the chimp can remove branches or leaves from the twig so it will go down a hole.

Rocks are used as tools by some chimps in West Africa to crack open nuts. Even weapon use is rather common among chimps, who use heavy branches as clubs.

However, none of these animal tools would be recognized as tools if they were found lying on the ground—they would just be sticks or rocks. What makes the tools used by humans and their ancestors different is that they show signs of being intentionally worked for particular purposes.

Rocks break by themselves all the time, such as when subjected to the alternation of hot days and freezing nights. Most of these broken rocks would be of little use to early humans, but a few (by chance) might have sharp edges that make usable blades. While it is impossible to know how human ancestors first thought of the idea of tools (perhaps 2 million years ago), one can imagine one of them examining one of the useful rocks and realizing that other rocks could be deliberately broken to create such an edge.

Since the most primitive tools would not look much different from ordinary broken rocks, the older are the possible tools, the more controversy there is likely to be about their nature. Evidence that rocks are actually tools might include similarities in structure to known types of tools or the presence of animal bones that have been cut in ways that suggest the use of sharp blades rather than, for example, the teeth of predators.

museum. Louis was "delighted beyond words." Loveridge encouraged the young man to continue looking for tools and to make records of where he found them. In other words, he showed him the beginnings of how to become involved with *archaeology.* As he also recounted in *White African,* he now "embarked on a study of the Stone Age in East Africa."

Consider what Louis had done. Some people—even archaeologists—had gone to Africa and, standing in a field with obsidian tools all around them, declared that there was nothing of interest—nothing made of flint! Louis, however, did not know that tools "had" to be made of flint. When he saw the shapes of the obsidian artifacts, he could imagine how an early human might have held and used them. Looking beneath the surface, he found "toolness." The ability to see the essential pattern or form in seemingly different objects or situations is a hallmark of the most creative scientists.

A SECOND EDUCATION

By 1919 the Great War (World War I) had ended. The 16-year-old Louis could finally go to England in search of a more advanced education. In many ways, he was far more experienced than the British boys of his age. After all, he spoke languages that few white people had mastered, and he could survive in conditions that the private school students could scarcely have imagined. On the other hand, Louis did not have the European cultural background that was expected of a boy his age. The whole panorama of British and European literature and art was as unknown to him as a jungle might be to his new classmates. His writing and speaking skills were equally rudimentary. Further, Louis simply looked and acted differently than his new classmates. His English had a curious overlay of Kikuyu rhythms. He even walked like a Kikuyu, putting one foot almost directly in front of the other, the way people would walk on a narrow African forest path.

Elite British schools of this type featured a system of hazing where the older students systematically humiliated younger students. The fact that Louis appeared to be so different just made him more of a target. The very day he arrived at school some boys locked him in a coal bin. He was teased unmercifully because he had no idea how to play cricket. They also found he could not swim—that being a skill of little use since there were no large bodies of water near Kabete in Kenya. In *White African,* Louis states that this sort of treatment "made me feel rather like an animal that had been wounded, and with which the herd would have nothing to do in consequence of its helplessness."

Further, the whole highly organized system of society in England was greatly constricting to someone who was used to hunting, exploring, or playing on an impromptu schedule. In *White African,* Louis recalls that unlike the freedom of his little African hut, at school he had to "go to bed at a given hour whether I was tired or not." In general, he said, "It was all very stupid from my point of view. I was being treated like a child of ten when I felt like a child of twenty, and it made me very bitter."

PREPARING FOR COLLEGE

The purpose of a preparatory school such as Weymouth was to enable the student to go on to one of Britain's prestigious universities. In Louis's case, the goal was Cambridge University. When Louis asked the headmaster at Weymouth about his prospects for the Cambridge entrance exams, he was discouraging despite Louis showing his enthusiasm by asking for permission to stay up past bedtime to study. When Louis asked about how to proceed after graduation, the headmaster, as reported in *White African,* "simply shrugged his shoulders" and suggested Louis try to find a job as a bank clerk. As Louis recounted in *White African,* such a lack of help or interest made him "utterly miserable."

However, his determination to succeed overcame any depression. Louis said, "I felt convinced in my own mind that if I tried hard enough, I could find a way of achieving what I wanted."

Louis turned to a more sympathetic source for help. His English teacher, Mr. Tunstall, was a Cambridge graduate and was impressed with Louis's potential and determination. He provided Louis with letters of recommendation, and in 1922, the 19-year-old Louis set off to Cambridge for interviews. He also took the entrance exams. In addition to passing Latin and French, he offered Kikuyu as his third language. There was no one at Cambridge qualified to examine Louis in Kikuyu, but he obtained letters certifying his proficiency in the language—one of them from a Kikuyu chief.

Louis was not only accepted to Cambridge, he even won a small scholarship.

CAMBRIDGE LIFE

With barely enough money to pay his basic expenses, Louis launched into his college career. He showed considerable ingenuity in supplementing his meager funds. In addition to working over the summer as a cook and

New Court, St. Johns College, Cambridge University. Attending this prestigious British institution represented quite a culture shock for Louis Leakey, who considered himself to be a White African. (kpzfoto-Alamy)

housekeeper, he obtained a grant from a missionary association (intended for children of missionaries who were also planning to enter the mission field). Later, he arranged to obtain dozens of ebony walking sticks from Kenyan woodcarvers and traded them for clothes and other necessities.

After having been confined in the strict world of the preparatory school, the considerable personal freedom offered by Cambridge must have come as a breath of fresh air. He had his own room and could come and go as he pleased.

Some students were fascinated by Louis's knowledge of Africa, while others made patronizing or even racist comments. One time, some students challenged Louis's statement that African villages miles apart could communicate by drum signals. Louis had several friends wait at various distances around the university and town of Cambridge. He then got up on the dorm roof with his drum and pounded on it. The booms, deafening nearby, could indeed be heard for miles. As the Cambridge officials sent watchmen in search of the source of the sound, Louis calmly took the drum back down to his room and put some cups on it, disguising it as a table!

Athletics were a big factor in Cambridge life. Louis joined the rugby team in his second year. (While not exactly an athlete, Louis's wiry strength served him well at this rough-and-tumble sport.) Unfortunately, during a key match Louis was accidentally kicked in the head. Showing the British stiff upper lip spirit, he shrugged off the injury and returned to the game, only to be injured again.

The next day Louis had a terrible headache—probably the result of a severe concussion. The doctors diagnosed him with posttraumatic epilepsy. Epilepsy can be a very difficult condition even today, depending on the severity and frequency of the symptoms, which can include migraine head-aches, blackouts, seizures, and depression. There is still no cure, and at that time there were no effective drug treatments. All the doctors could recom-mend was that Louis take a year off from college and find a quiet place to rest and recover. Louis had no money for an extra year. (Fortunately, although the headaches would return periodically, the symptoms were not enough to permanently interfere with Louis's future work.)

DINOSAUR HUNT

Searching for some sort of job for his time away from school, Louis learned from a family friend that the British Museum of Natural History was organizing an expedition to Tendaguru in Tanganyika Territory (now Tanzania) to hunt for dinosaur skeletons. Before the war, a German scien-tist had found a huge *Brachiosaurus* fossil. By the 1920s, dinosaurs were becoming a popular craze among natural history museums. The British, having acquired control of the former German territory through a League of Nations mandate, saw an opportunity to acquire some big dinosaurs of their own.

The expedition's leader, the well-known dinosaur hunter W. E. Cutler, had a problem: He knew little about Africa and did not speak any African language. Although young, Louis already had extensive experience with Africa's people, animals, and landscape. Cutler hired him as his assistant, and in March 1924 the expedition landed at Mombasa, Kenya, and headed overland to Tanganyika.

From the very beginning, Cutler had to depend on Louis's experience and resourcefulness. The Tendaguru site was hard to find on maps and had to be pinned down. While Cutler remained in Dar es Salaam and read up on *geology,* Louis, with the aid of Jumbe Ismaeli, a village chief, organized a tra-ditional African safari—including 15 porters, a gun-bearer, and a cook. At the head of the column marched Louis, on what (in *White African*) he would call "a great adventure."

The overland journey took three days and covered 56 miles (90.1 km). When they finally found the site, Jumbe told Louis to fire his rifle into the air. That, along with drum signals, told the natives in the area that there was work to be had. Soon a group of grass huts ringed the camp. Two months later, Louis went back to fetch Cutler, and the two proceeded to the camp with a new flock of porters and supplies.

Cutler had energy, courage, and self-assurance. Unfortunately, he also thought he knew everything one needed to know and tended to ignore Louis's advice. As a small example, when he started rubbing a certain sort of seed pod, Louis told him that if he continued he would start to itch and burn. Cutler put some of the pods in his handkerchief and then absentmindedly used the same handkerchief to wipe the sweat off his arms and thighs. Suddenly he leaped up (as reported in *White African*) "yelling like a madman and cursing like a trooper."

The actual work proceeded despite Leakey being frequently laid low by malaria, that great curse of the tropics. Cutler's field diary, as quoted by Virginia Morrell in *Ancestral Passions,* had entries such as these:

> Leakey very low with malaria, temperature 104 . . . Leakey still has malarial symptoms . . . but he superintended ditches 4, 5, and 6 all day. Cutler, too, reported that he was "passing blood and vomiting."

The ditches or trenches were the only way they could excavate the largest dinosaur bones. The bones were very fragile and had to be quickly preserved in plaster. Cutler, an expert in such techniques, would not let Louis join in this work. Nevertheless, the observant Louis watched closely and, in his book *Adam's Ancestors,* later acknowledged that

> [Cutler's knowledge] of the technique of excavating and preserving fossil bones was unsurpassed. . . . I learned more about the technical side of the search and preservation of fossil bones [from him] than I could have gleaned from a far longer period of theoretical study.

Overall, the dinosaur hunt was rather disappointing. There turned out not to be any complete dinosaurs in the area. Nevertheless, the trip was Leakey's true baptism as a field paleontologist.

PUBLIC DEBUT AND GRADUATION

Louis tried to get Cambridge to extend his time in Africa, but the authorities insisted he return to complete his studies. Cutler, who had learned enough Swahili to communicate with the African workers, stayed on. Although he gave Leakey permission to give lectures about the expedition in order to earn some money for college, Cutler worried that Leakey would get all the publicity and perhaps steal all the glory.

For Leakey, the challenge waiting in Cambridge was daunting. Louis had no experience speaking in public and, as he notes in *White African:* "As I was only an undergraduate in my second year, and not yet twenty-two years old, and never having lectured in public before, I grew more and more worried as the day approached."

When the day came, Louis looked out over a group that included formidable Cambridge professors and museum officials. Even his borrowed, poorly fitting formal clothes added to his discomfort. As he began to speak, however, Louis gradually became calmer. The lecture was a success, and Louis found that he had a knack for storytelling. Certainly there were numerous tales he could tell—such as the time he kept a baby baboon in his hut as a pet. One night while Louis was asleep, a leopard sneaked into the room, grabbed the baboon, and leaped out through the window! Throughout the rest of his career, Louis would frequently go on the road to raise money for upcoming expeditions or projects. His fund of stories made the whole business of *paleontology* seem glamorous and exotic—and would turn Leakey into something of a rock star, to the irritation of more conventional colleagues.

TURNING TO ANTHROPOLOGY

The most important outcome of Louis's first African expedition was his decision that he wanted to be an anthropologist rather than a missionary. However, he first had to graduate, and the question of his third qualifying language, Kikuyu, came up again. For graduation, Cambridge insisted on a direct examination, not a mere letter or certificate. Cambridge had trouble finding a British expert in Kikuyu. Well, there was one . . . soon Louis received a letter from Cambridge asking him if he would be willing to examine a Cambridge student in Kikuyu! Since examining oneself would not do, it was agreed that Louis's academic adviser would examine him, though the latter had actually learned most of his Kikuyu from Louis.

During his final years at Cambridge, Louis had been fortunate to be able to study with Alfred Cort Haddon (1855–1940), a pioneering British anthropologist. Specializing in the culture of New Guinea, Haddon always made time to help students seeking a career in *anthropology*. In addition to practical advice, Louis picked up an odd pastime from Haddon. The older anthropologist had studied the complex figures people in some cultures created from string. (A simple version is the game Cat's Cradle that used to be popular with children in the time before video games.) Later, Louis would often carry some string in his pocket, ready to intrigue a child or grownup with an interesting figure.

Back at Cambridge, Louis moved toward graduation, exhibiting new confidence. In his final exams in anthropology and archaeology he earned double firsts—the highest honors. It had been quite a journey from a 12-year-old's fascination with the prehistoric world to graduation from one of the world's greatest universities. As Louis noted in *White African,* "The dreams I had dreamed as a child after reading Hall's *Days Before History* were coming true."

Launching a Career

In June 1926, Louis received his bachelor's degree, along with a research fellowship to enable him to lead an East African archaeological expedition. Additional backing came in the form of grants from the Royal Society (Britain's most prestigious scientific organization), the Percy Sladen Memorial Trust, and even the colonial government of Kenya. This amounted to a remarkable vote of confidence for a young scientist just out of school. Equally, though, it would mean that he would have to meet high expectations.

Where to begin? Louis decided to start with the land he knew best, the Kikuyu country of his youth. As a teenager, he and his sisters had, with the help of two Kikuyu men, explored a cave near a waterfall they had called Gibberish. They had found nothing but a single flake of obsidian, but at the time it had not occurred to them to dig into the ground.

Now, in summer 1926, it would be different. Louis, along with fellow Cambridge student Bernard Newsom and two elderly Kikuyu dug a trench down the center of the cave and then worked their way under the floor. Numerous obsidian tools started to appear, much to the daily fascination of local Kikuyu. (The natives, however, were not pleased at the prospect of digging up human bones, which they believed would belong to a tribe of pygmylike people who had lived there before them.)

SEARCH FOR THE HAND AX PEOPLE

Ultimately, though, Louis was searching for something before the age of obsidian flakes—signs of whatever culture had made the earliest hand axes, large pear-shaped rocks with edges strong enough to split large bones. At the time, scientists had little idea how long ago such tools first began to be made, let alone who might have made them.

Knowledge of the age of life and the Earth itself was in transition. By the 1920s, the scientific consensus was that humanlike creatures probably dated back no more than about 200,000 years. Mammals as a whole were believed to go back perhaps 3 million years, and the Earth itself was supposed to be about 65 million years old. (The corresponding ages as known today are about 3–4 million years for the first human ancestors. The Cenozoic, or Age of Mammals, began about 65 million years ago, and the Earth itself is known to be about 4.5 billion years old.)

Louis failed to find these older *Chellean* (now called *Oldowan*) tools at Gibberish cave. Indeed, no one had yet found hand axes anywhere in East Africa. Undaunted, as he would later say in *Adam's Ancestors,* Louis "argued to myself that if only I could find the right places in which to search, I must be able to find this oldest culture in East Africa too."

Back when he was a teenager, Louis had heard a talk by J. W. Gregory, a geologist who had been the first person to discover stone tools in East Africa. Gregory had mentioned a site on the shore of Lake Elmenteita as a possible source of such tools. Now, on his return as a trained archaeologist, Louis noticed a skull sticking out of a crack in the face of a cliff. Digging a small trench, he went on to find some human and animal bones, together with bits of pottery.

Louis and Newsom set up their camp in a "large and airy" structure in an abandoned farm. (It was actually a former pigsty.) Beginning work in January 1927, they unearthed more than two dozen skeletons, obsidian tools, and pottery. Trying to fit the finds into his growing mental map of African prehistory, he concluded that the people who had made these tools and pottery (whom he dubbed the Elmenteitans) had lived prior to the Kikuyu's ancestors, deeper in the Stone Age—but still, they were not the ancient stone ax makers.

As word of the excavations spread via a local newspaper, a nearby farmer named Gamble offered Louis the opportunity to investigate two caves on his property. In preliminary excavations, they found more bones and tools, with the promise of older, deeper layers to come.

VISITING LADIES

One day Louis and his crew had some unusual visitors. They were two young women from Cambridge—Janet Forbes and Henrietta Wilfrida ("Frida") Avern. Bored with settled life, they had launched on a sort of madcap African odyssey, setting out by steamer to Mombasa, where they bought a box-body (a sort of small truck) and hired a Masai as guide.

Louis invited the two women to his "airy" sty for dinner. As told in an interview quoted in *Ancestral Passions,* Frida found that

> The supper table was covered with stone tools before we had anything to eat. There was a python skin drying outside in the sun, and bones and stones covering everything inside. And Louis talked absolutely nonstop about stratified sites and dating. I think he was probably starving for a little reasonably shared and intelligent conversation, and an audience. We talked archaeology until dawn.

Frida particularly impressed Louis. She was bright, energetic, and a student of many fields, including archaeology. In turn, she was fascinated by the stories Louis wove about how the land had changed through the ages and how the most ancient Africans might have lived.

Louis soon found he was in love with Frida. The following day, when it was time to see the ladies off on their train back to Nairobi, Louis spoke to Frida through the train window, suggesting that they get married when both had returned to England.

DIGGING IN GAMBLE'S CAVE

Frida was not quite ready to make that sort of commitment based on a few day's acquaintance, but Louis and Frida were married a year later, in July 1928. They then returned to Gamble's cave, where Frida soon became a full-fledged member of the expedition. However, tramping in the African bush with a young archaeologist was probably not what Frida's parents (respectable British merchants) had in mind for their daughter. As described in a letter by Elisabeth Kitson (a newly acquired member of the team) to her father (quoted in *Ancestral Passions*) the camp

> . . . consists of a collection of huts made of wattle & daub with thatched roofs, all in a *very* doubtful state of repair & cleanliness. The furniture (such as there is) is made of packing cases & there is a barbed wire entanglement across every window instead of glass. . . . The bedroom part is just like a cowshed—there's no ceiling but just the bare rafter poles & thatch above . . . full of bats & crickets & spiders & doubtless other unknown horrors. The walls are just partitions & don't go up to the top so you can

have conversations with your next door neighbor or the person in the bath. The floor is just bare earth.

The camp was surrounded by the huts of young Kikuyu, many of whom had been the boys he had grown up with. Meanwhile, generous funding from a number of sources had allowed him to hire more people to join the team, including his brother Douglas and a young friend of Frida's named Penelope Jenkins.

Most of the newcomers were greenhorns who knew little about life in the African bush. This gave an opportunity for Louis's mischievous side. First, he explained to the new arrivals that they might well encounter lions or rhinos—but not to fear, since he had his trusty rifle. Suddenly, the group heard the roar of a lion, followed by natives running about and men grabbing guns. Louis said a lion had just gone past the camp. The next day, however, Louis cheerfully revealed that it had all been an elaborate hoax—the lion was just some creative sound effects.

Louis constantly showed initiative and resourcefulness, sometimes in startling ways. When Elisabeth Kitson developed a painful boil, it seemed beyond the capabilities of such first aid supplies as they had. But then Louis took a sharp obsidian flake and lanced it.

A restless imagination distinguished Louis from the more methodical scientist who would never venture forth with a *theory* until every possible objection had been answered. For example, when excavation uncovered a pile of obsidian chips seemingly too small to be any sort of tool, Louis concluded that they were the barbs from a fish harpoon.

As lively as Louis could be around the sorting table or at supper, the work was a serious matter, and it went on steadily. Uncovering layers by careful digging, sifting, and sorting, each layer represented an earlier time than the previous one. As Leakey recalls in *Adam's Ancestors*

> We were gradually working backwards [in time], and so my hopes were strengthened that one day, sooner or later, I would find traces of the oldest known types of stone tool, and possibly even the bones of the men who made them.

What kept driving Louis on in a search for earlier and earlier human fossils and tools? One team member, John Solomon, would recall many years later in a letter to Virginia Morrell quoted in *Ancestral Passions* that

> Nobody could possibly fail to notice Louis's fanatical adherence to the belief that the human genus first emerged in tropical Africa. This belief

might be regarded as "religious" rather than "scientific," and he eagerly grasped at any datum which might corroborate it.

The result, according to Solomon, was that Louis always tried "to attribute the maximum possible antiquity" to any human fossil or artifact.

Over all, the excavations at Elmenteita (and particularly Gamble's cave) in 1928 and 1929 were quite successful. Louis and his team had found two human skeletons and an impressive collection of stone tools. The most important discovery came almost at the very end of their stay at Elmenteita—a group of pear-shaped stone axes found at a place called Kariandusi. Finding this oldest form of tool lent weight to Louis's belief that the earliest humans came from Africa. Louis would later write in *White African* that "The discovery was . . . of the very greatest importance, as it threw entirely new light on the age of the Great Rift Valley." Louis was more right than he knew. While he estimated the tools he had found were from an ice age between 40,000 and 50,000 years ago, modern methods reveal them to be more than 10 times older—about 500,000 years ago.

TRIUMPHANT RETURN

It was time to report on the group's exciting findings. The first opportunity was to be the 1929 annual meeting of the British Association for the Advancement of Science, which was to be held in Capetown, South Africa. The journey south was not an easy one (there was no air travel yet). They would have to drive 3,000 miles (4,828 km) down something called the Great North Road. At the time, the road was not good and in many places it was hardly a road at all, barely a trail. When the party arrived in Johannesburg, a newspaper headline read "From Kenya Colony by Truck/Archaeologists Venture /on [1 pound] a Day Each."

Prior to the meeting, Louis's mentor Alfred Cort Haddon, who had heard rumors of Louis's finds, struck a cautionary note. As later recounted in the book *Leakey's Luck*, he urged Louis to "be careful what you say. Naturally, you will tell them of what you have found, but do not go in for wild hypotheses. These won't do your work any good and it's foolish to try to make a splash."

Unlike some later times in his career, Louis seems to have taken this advice. He reported his findings in a businesslike report titled "An Outline of the Stone Age in Kenya." Kenya was now definitely on the archaeological map, and the question of how far back African prehistory went was a lively and controversial one. After returning to the camp in Kenya, Louis would host several parties of visiting scientists, explaining to them how and where the finds had been made and their geological context.

Finally, in November 1929, Louis and Frida sailed back to England, where a two-year fellowship and a comfortable little cottage awaited them at Cambridge.

THINKING ABOUT OLDUVAI

The question of the age of the earliest humans continued to be a vexing one. To Louis, the new human skeletons he had found in Gamble's cave looked to

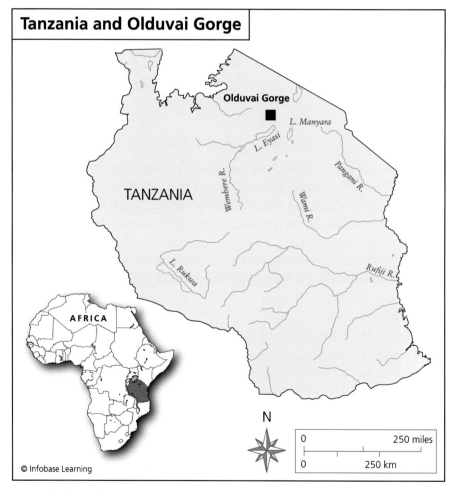

A map that shows the location of Olduvai Gorge in the east African nation of Tanzania, not far from Kenya.

LEAKEY'S DRAWING MACHINE

As Louis began to work on a companion volume, *The Stone Age Races of Kenya*, he ran into a problem. Skulls were more complicated to illustrate than tools. To keep the proper scale and proportion for a drawing, many exacting measurements would be required. Doing these by hand might consume many hours. (Photography, while valuable in some applications, was not an adequate substitute for drawings, which could bring out the most essential features of a specimen.)

One day, a mechanically talented friend named J. Harper suggested that Louis design some sort of machine to help make the drawings. The resourceful Louis decided that this was a great idea, and the two men set to work. The eventual device was something like an elaborate version of the drafting tables used by engineers and architects in precomputer days. It consisted of wires, cables, screws, and wheels connecting numerous drawing pens. With the aid of the device, drawings could be automatically scaled from one size to another.

The device, called the Leakey-Harper drawing machine, was patented and reported on in the August 1930 issue of the scientific journal *Nature*. A British instrument company undertook to manufacture the machine. While it is uncertain how many were sold, it is known that the Royal College of Surgeons used one for medical illustrations and another one ended up somewhere in Japan.

be about the same anatomically as the Olduvai Man that Hans Reck had found in the Olduvai Gorge back in 1913. The geological and archaeological evidence at the Gamble's cave site pointed to the Middle Stone Age (a few tens of thousands of years old). However, Reck still insisted that Olduvai Man was about half a million years old.

Louis went to Berlin and discussed the dating issue with Reck. Reck adamantly insisted on the older date, but he also eagerly agreed to join the new Olduvai expedition Louis was planning. Reck brought out his extensive collection of rocks and fossils that he had collected at Olduvai, and the two archaeologists pored over them as they began to make plans. At one point, Louis noticed something that looked a lot like one of the stone hand axes from Kariandusi. He then, as noted in *White African*, told Reck that "I was now certain in my own mind that the greater part of the [Olduvai] . . . deposit was probably of the same age as the beds in the Kariandusi River . . . and I expressed the opinion that we should find implements of this culture at [Olduvai]." Reck was doubtful: He said he had looked for stone tools but had found only animal fossils. Louis proposed a bet that he would find Stone Age tools at Olduvai within 24 hours of their arrival, and Reck accepted.

Back at Cambridge and London, Louis had numerous meetings with people to gain backing for the expedition. St. John's College of Cambridge was enthusiastic about their prodigious former student. The college provided another fellowship and a lab, along with rooms where Louis could stay when he was immersed in his work. Meanwhile, Frida stayed home in their cottage, carefully sketching stone tools to illustrate what would become Louis's first book, *The Stone Age Cultures of Kenya Colony.* When they were together, husband and wife seemed devoted to one another as well as to their shared work.

SCOUTING THE GORGE

In July 1931, Louis arrived back in Kenya. To save money (which was nearly always tight), Louis disembarked the steamer at Mombasa, then drove the 350 miles (563 km) to Nairobi rather than taking the train. His parents had retired as missionaries the previous year and had bought a small farm in Limuru, in the highlands about 18 miles (29 km) from Nairobi. Arriving there, he went to work building a hut for his own family, described in *White African* as having a corrugated iron roof, a packed earth floor, but with "proper doors and windows." The cost was all of 36 pounds.

Olduvai Gorge is about 260 miles (418 km) south of Nairobi. While it may look ancient and unchanging, Olduvai is the product of a great deal of geologic activity, including volcanic eruptions (creating lava and ash) and layer upon layer of sediment, ideal for burying and preserving fossils. What nature hides it can also reveal, and about 500,000 years ago seismic activity diverted a nearby stream, which began to cut through the layers of sediment. Today, five main layers, or "beds," going back about 2 million years are laid open to the efforts of several generations of researchers.

According to a legend often recounted by Louis, in 1911 the German entomologist Wilhelm Kattwinkel was chasing a rare butterfly. Before he could net it, he tumbled off a rocky ledge. When he recovered his senses, Kattwinkel looked around and saw many layers of sediment out of which protruded a profusion of fossils. However he might have actually found Olduvai, Kattwinkel collected some fossils there, and the find inspired Hans Reck to organize an expedition to the site. Reck collected 1,700 fossils but claimed there were no tools.

As he learned more about Olduvai, Louis decided that it would be a good place for his first full-fledged expedition in search of early humans and their tools. Hans Reck accompanied him.

There was a road for the first 110 miles (177 km), then a sort of track, and then the Serengeti Plain. This vast golden grassland, broken by washes (gullies cut by streams), featured great herds of antelope, zebra, giraffe, and other animals—and the numerous lions that preyed on them. To guard against the latter, Louis hired an experienced hunter-guide to guard the little caravan of three trucks and one car. There were no settlements in Olduvai where supplies might be replenished—everything they would need for the season would have to be brought, except for meat they could obtain by hunting.

When they finally arrived at the campsite, they were dust-covered and exhausted, yet they had to begin an urgent quest for drinkable water. Nevertheless Reck was delighted at having finally been able to return to the scene of his former discoveries. Louis, meanwhile, later recalled in *White African* that he was torn between "awful visions of a sudden and tragic conclusion" to the expedition and the "prospect of great discoveries at [Olduvai]."

THE FIRST SEASON AT OLDUVAI

They were soon off to a good start. After some initial fumbling, Reck was able to relocate the exact site where he had found Olduvai Man almost 20 years earlier. Louis and his team found 77 hand axes in just four days, easily winning his 10-pound bet with Reck that he would find tools within the first 24 hours. (Reck had not recognized the hand axes as tools because they were not made of flint, but of volcanic rock and quartz.)

As they examined the site, they noted the five distinct layers or beds. Reck pointed to where he said Olduvai Man had been found, insisting that it had been buried in Bed II (the second oldest). Reck argued that because the layer above the skeleton had not been disturbed, the fossil must have been buried hundreds of thousands of years ago.

When he saw the skeleton in Germany, Louis had been skeptical of Reck's claims for its great antiquity. Anatomically, it looked too much like the more modern humans he had examined, such as the Stone Age ones at Gamble's cave. However, Louis allowed himself to be convinced by Reck, and

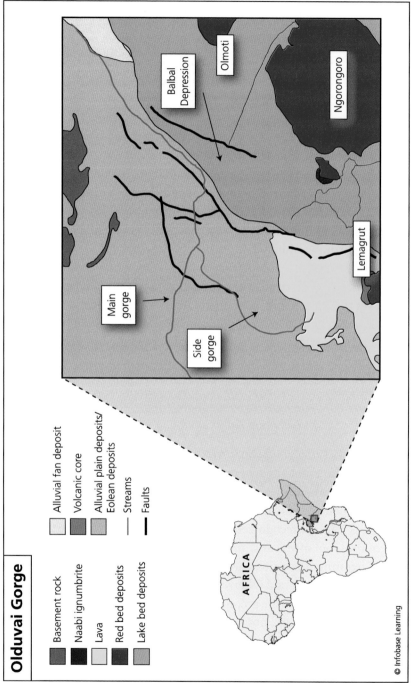

Olduvai Gorge

Basement rock
Naabi ignumbrite
Lava
Red bed deposits
Lake bed deposits

Alluvial fan deposit
Volcanic core
Alluvial plain deposits/
Eolean deposits
— Streams
— Faults

Balbal
Depression

Olmoti

Ngorongoro

Lemagrut

Main
gorge

Side
gorge

AFRICA

© Infobase Learning

The rich fossil beds at Olduvai Gorge were the result of multiple layers of sediment being laid down over the course of several million years around a now-vanished lake. This chart shows the major geological regions at Olduvai.

together they drafted a letter to *Nature* proclaiming that Olduvai Man was the oldest known human. With an age of half a million years, the find also seemed to lend great strength to the argument that humans had originated not in Europe or Asia but in Africa. That letter was quickly followed by others sent to Haddon as well as Sir Arthur Keith (1866–1955), an eminent British anthropologist and anatomist. There were also reports to African newspapers and to the *Times* (London). Headlines and news quickly spread around the globe: The oldest known skeleton of modern humans, *Homo sapiens,* had been verified.

As the season drew to an end, however, many puzzles remained. Tools had been found even as far down as Bed I, the oldest layer in the gorge. These hand axes seemed more primitive than those found earlier at Kariandusi. In *Adam's Ancestors,* Louis described them as consisting of "a pebble or lump of rock roughly trimmed to a cutting edge along one side." He attributed these tools as belonging to the (as yet unknown) Oldowan culture. But where were the remains of their maker? Despite the intensive search, no new human skeletons had been found. There was only the Olduvai Man, the one they now claimed was 500,000 years old. Louis did not think this modern-looking human would have made such primitive tools.

SEARCHING FOR PROOF

It turned out that the doubts that had tugged at Louis's mind would soon be expressed openly in the scientific community. John Solomon, a geologist who had helped Louis's expedition to Elmenteita, had developed a new chemical test for identifying the minerals in sedimentary deposits such as the five main beds at Olduvai. When Solomon tested a scraping from inside the rib of Reck's Olduvai Man skeleton, it included a particular crystalline form of volcanic mineral that was not to be found in a sample of the material in Bed II. This suggested the skeleton had not been originally buried and fossilized in that ancient layer. Perhaps it had later shifted down into Bed II (erosion, seismic shifts, or other movements can jumble fossils from one layer into another). Perhaps Reck had simply misremembered the location of the find and the skeleton never was in Bed II at all. At any rate, its age was again open to doubt.

Louis was angry and accused Solomon of slipshod technique. At any rate, he wrote to Sir Arthur Keith (who had supported Louis, but now expressed doubts) that (all in caps) "I WANT IF POSSIBLE TO FIND ANOTHER [OLDUVAI] SKELTON." He thought that if he reexplored one of the caves in which he had already found Olduvai-type animal fossils and stone tools, he might find such a skeleton and then "perhaps I should be able to convince you all!"

One area that seemed to be promising was a site at Kanjera, a few miles from the shore of Lake Victoria in western Kenya, a site that had rich fossil beds. In March 1932, Louis set up camp at Kanjera. He immediately found fossils from extinct elephants and stone tools, both similar to those they had found in Olduvai. On the second day, they found some skull fragments that had been washed out of exposed rock. Louis was convinced the human fragments had been fossilized in the same way as the previous day's finds, suggesting similar age. Gradually, as they pieced together the fragments of what turned out to be two skulls, they had enough to identify them as *H. sapiens*. Writing to Arthur Hopwood, he noted that this latest find "will be a bit of a blow to the 'Anti-Olodway-Man' group!"

Louis knew, however, that some skull fragments washed away from an unknown site would not be enough to satisfy the critics. For the paleontologist, the gold standard was a fossil found *in situ*, that is, in the place where it had originally formed. Louis continued the search, hampered by heavy rains and swarms of mosquitoes. He also decided to explore a nearby site called Kanam.

They began to find fossils including the *mandible* of an extinct pig. A little later, a fragment of rock revealed some unmistakably human premolar teeth. Picking away the rock revealed part of a jaw that had been badly weathered. It convinced Louis that he had found proof at last, as described later in *Adam's Ancestors*, "a man who was a true ancestor of *Homo sapiens*." After photographing the site, he marked it with four iron pegs set into concrete. Back at Kanjera, Louis eventually found more skull fragments, all apparently in situ in sediment similar to that of Olduvai Bed II.

Back in England, geologists continued to undermine the original Olduvai Man. They eventually determined that part of Bed II had been exposed in comparatively recent times and the skeleton buried then. Subsequent erosion had led to a confusion of layers, but in fact Olduvai Man was no older than the Stone Age skeletons of Elmenteita. (Later carbon-14 tests would give a date of about 19,000 years.)

In letters quoted in *Ancestral Passions,* Louis, writing to Miles Burkitt, insisted that

Everyone insists that *Homo sapiens* must go back to the beginning of the Pleistocene—at least—somewhere. The question has always been 'Where?' And the evidence . . . seems to suggest that the answer is 'the region of the great central African lakes.'

However, as Louis wrote to Arthur Hopwood shortly before returning home, "I can foresee great fights when I get back."

Triumph and Disaster

In November 1932, Louis and Frida returned to England. By then, they had a daughter, Priscilla. The grants had run out, and the only money they had left was Frida's dowry. They bought a small house known as The Close. It was pleasant enough: a sprawling brick house with a nice garden, surrounded by green fields. This idyllic rural village setting was only three miles from Cambridge, making for an easy bicycle ride for Louis (who had been provided with a suite of rooms at St. John's). Fortunately, Louis's fellowship was then renewed, and they had just about enough money to get by.

Louis in fact spent most of his time at the college, working on a vast array of stone tools from Olduvai and the fossils from Kanjera and Kanam. Louis used two rooms for storing, sorting, and studying his specimens. The third room was, as described in Leakey's memoir *By the Evidence:*

> a combined emergency bedroom, kitchen, and dining room. . . . The great advantage of this arrangement was that when I worked late in to the night, as I often did, I could sleep in college and cook breakfast next morning, instead of having to . . . disturb my family in the middle of the night.

Meanwhile, the controversy over the age of human fossils in East Africa raged on. Louis finally had to admit that the evidence showed that Olduvai Man was a recent Stone Age specimen. Nevertheless, he continued to insist that the jaw fragment he had found at Kanam really was from the middle of the *Pleistocene*, hundreds of thousands of years ago.

Hopwood had warned Louis that for the Kanam find to "hold up," he would have to prove that it really had been found in situ—an exact location combined with geological evidence that there had not been some sort of shift. If, said his letter to Leakey quoted in *Ancestral Passions*, "you have plenty of evidence, checked and cross-checked, there will be eventual triumph for you."

A STAMP OF APPROVAL

In March 1933, a special meeting of the Royal Anthropological Institute was convened to discuss the evidence from Kanam and Kanjera. In his preparation, Louis was helped by a strong supporter, Sir Arthur Keith, who shared a belief in the antiquity of modern *H. sapiens*. The opponents were led by Percy George Hamnall Boswell (1886–1960), a noted geologist and expert on the Pleistocene. Boswell had seen how badly flawed the geological evidence at Olduvai had been. He also believed it unlikely that humans would evolve so slowly that there would be little visible difference between a supposed half a million year old skull and its modern counterpart. Unlike the wide-ranging, intuitive (and sometimes a bit slapdash) approach of Louis, Boswell believed in slow, meticulous analysis. One could say their theoretical differences were matched by a difference in personal style.

In general, the evaluation committee sided with Louis, urging only that he obtain some additional geological evidence. Louis was praised for his work, and the media in turn reported a momentous discovery. The *Times* (London) of October 21, 1933, noted that Louis's findings meant that "plausibility is . . . lent to the theory, first advanced by Darwin, that Africa is the cradle of the human race." In October 1933, Louis gave the species represented by the Kanam jaw the name *Homo kanamensis*. This meant that he thought it was of the same *genus (Homo)* as modern people, but represented an earlier species.

With such an official stamp of approval in place, Leakey's future career looked bright. The Royal Society asked Louis to exhibit the Kanam jaw in the British Museum of Natural History. The London publisher Methuen offered a contract for Louis to write a popular book about his discoveries; it would be published as *Adam's Ancestors*. In it, he would portray the human ancestor represented by the Kanam jaw as being on the direct line of descent leading to modern humanity.

At a dinner in Louis's honor arranged by the fellows of the Royal Anthropological Institute, an archaeologist named Gertrude Caton-Thompson sat nearby, accompanied by a remarkable young woman Mary Nicol.

MARY'S BEGINNINGS

Mary Nicol was born on February 6, 1913, in London, England. Her father, Erskine Nicol, was a painter specializing in landscapes, so the family traveled frequently, going to France, Italy, and Egypt to paint scenes. (Mary's mother, Cecilia Frere, had also studied art in Italy.)

Mary began to draw when she was about 10 years old. While she received no formal artistic training, she must have had many opportunities to watch her father work. Erskine was interested in archaeology and took the family to the Dordogne region of France. He encouraged his daughter to look for flint tools and even took her to see the famous cave paintings made by people between about 35,000 and 10,000 years ago. There was also a museum nearby at Les Eyzies, which had tools and other artifacts from Stone Age people. When Mary's parents became friends with the archaeologist at the museum, Mary and her father were allowed to visit his excavation site. Mary was even permitted to keep any tools she found after he had taken those he wanted to keep.

In her autobiography *Disclosing the Past,* Mary recalls that as she examined and thought about her little collection of stone tools, "I remember wondering about the age of the pieces, and the world of their makers."

ART AND ARCHAEOLOGY

In childhood, Mary and her father had spent many happy days walking, looking for tools, or watching wild animals. Although Louis and his Kikuyu friends inhabited a quite different landscape, one can see how both Louis and Mary had grown up paying attention to the living world and the traces of the past.

Also, like Louis, Mary had little formal education—mainly due to the family's constant travels. After her father's sudden death (a shattering experience for her), Mary's mother did enroll her in a convent school. Her reaction to this formal environment was rather like Louis's. Compared to her father, the museum archaeologist, and the family's other adult friends, classmates of her own age seemed, as she notes in *Disclosing the Past,* "utterly juvenile compared to the company I was used to keeping."

MARY AND THE CAVE PAINTINGS

In 1935 (one might say during their courtship), Louis and Mary had first gone to two places in Tanganyika, Kondoa Irangi and Kisese, to see a spectacular group of rock paintings. At the time, Louis and Mary had promised one another they would return and make a serious study of them. A South African archaeologist named Van Riet Lowe had long studied rock paintings in both North and South Africa and noted considerable similarities. He encouraged the Leakeys to study the Tanganyika paintings to see how they, located in East Africa midway between the other two regions, might complete the overall picture of African prehistoric painting.

In 1951, having secured a grant of 2,000 pounds from the Wenner-Gren Foundation for Anthropological Research in New York, Louis and Mary, together with their boys and the now ever-present Dalmatian dogs, set out to work on the art study.

In *Disclosing the Past* Mary would note that

> Those three months at Kondoa Irangi . . . will always count as one of the highlights of my life and work in East Africa. . . . It was the combination—the beauty of the country, the beauty of the paintings, the fascination of disentangling the art, the feeling that we were achieving something by putting these paintings on record—all of that, and having the family there. It was great fun.

Unlike European art, which comes in discrete pieces, each composed according to some theme, the prehistoric rock paintings consisted of swarms of figures of animals and humans, sometime overlapping. Standing on a ladder, the Leakeys used cellophane paper and paint to make careful copies of as many of the figures as possible. (Mary, it should be recalled, first attracted Louis's attention through her skill as an artist and illustrator.)

While the work for which the Leakeys became famous was in paleontology and archaeology—fossils and artifacts—the episode with the cave paintings also shows their interest in anthropology and their desire to study human culture through its artistic expression.

Mary's adventurous and rebellious streak was soon evident. Indeed, she was dismissed from not one but two convent schools—one time, because she had figured out how to set off an explosion during a chemistry lesson! It was not that Mary could not learn. Rather, she wanted to learn only what interested her.

It eventually became clear that archaeology would be her passion. She met a British woman archaeologist named Dorothy Liddell. Her success suggested that women could enter the field and actually get somewhere. Soon

JOHN FRERE, PIONEER ARCHAEOLOGIST

Mary Nicol's family heritage also included a keen interest in the ancient world: Erskine was an amateur Egyptologist. Going all the way back to 1797, Mary's great-great-grandfather John Frere (1740–1807) had been the first person in England to recognize the significance of the flint tools that were often found while digging foundations.

In a letter to the Royal Society in London, Frere described how in a bricklayer's pit at a depth of about 12 feet (4 m) tools had been found, together with fossil bones of extinct animals. Frere carefully noted the separate layers or strata of rock between the surface and the area where the bones and tools were found. He realized that depositing these layers must have taken a considerable amount of time, measured in thousands of years.

In his letter he thus described the flint objects as

> . . . weapons of war, fabricated by a people who had not the use
> of metals . . . The situation in which these weapons were found
> may tempt us to refer them to a very remote period indeed, even
> beyond that of the present world.

At the time, Frere's bold *hypothesis* received little attention. It would not be recognized until 1830 when Charles Lyell (1797–1875) would publish his pioneering work in geology, explaining that the Earth was much older than the 6,000 years suggested by the Bible. The tools were dismissed as shards perhaps created by lightning bolts. Fossils, too, might have been wondered at but had not really been connected to anything living today. It would only be many years later that Frere would be recognized as an archaeological pioneer.

Mary was attending lectures at London museums and sitting in on classes in archaeology and geology at Oxford University. Mary's mother wanted her to go to Oxford, but they found that she had no chance since she had not actually earned any school diplomas.

Mary did have another way to get into the archaeological field—her talent for drawing. She began to write to archaeologists, asking whether she could work at their sites and prepare illustrations for their reports or books. In 1930, Dorothy Liddell did hire her as an assistant for her work at Hembury in Devon, England. For several years Mary worked with Dorothy, learning to excavate pottery, tools, and other artifacts. Dorothy asked Mary to draw some of the finds, and the drawings appeared in publications about the site.

When they were published, Mary's drawings came to the attention of another archaeologist, Gertrude Caton-Thompson, who was quite impressed with the quality of the work. She hired Mary to illustrate stone tools she had found in Egypt. Pleased with Mary's efforts there, Caton-Thompson invited her to attend a lecture at the Royal Anthropological Institute in London. The featured speaker was to be a young man who had found interesting tools and fossils in an exotic place called Olduvai in Africa. His name of course was Louis Leakey.

A NEW PARTNERSHIP

Louis and Mary apparently enjoyed their conversation. After seeing Mary's illustrations for Caton-Thompson's forthcoming book on Egyptian antiquities, he noted that her illustrations of stone tools were (as he would write in *By the Evidence*) "the best representations . . . I have ever seen." Mary's energy and wit also intrigued him. When Mary went off on an archaeological dig, he frequently wrote letters to her. When they met again at the end of the summer, a spark had clearly ignited.

As Mary wrote in her autobiography *Disclosing the Past:*

from the time we met up soon after our arrivals we became inseparable companions . . . and it was here I first felt and instinctively recognized something that was new to me: the mental stimulus and physical thrill of having Louis with me.

By the end of the conference, Mary recalled, "It was clearly understood between us that we would meet again, soon and frequently."

This was not the first time Louis had formed romantic attachments to women other than his wife. (The rooms at Cambridge could be convenient for activities besides work.) A number of Louis's friends had noticed how women seemed to gather around him in lively conversation. It soon became clear around Cambridge that Louis and Mary were a couple. Meanwhile, Frida seemed to be unaware of this side of her husband's character. She remained at The Close, raising their daughter Priscilla and about to have a second child.

The time came when Louis told Mary that he wanted to end his marriage to Frida and marry her. Finally, in January 1934, a month after the birth of their son, Colin, Louis told Frida that he was in love with Mary and wanted to take her to Africa with him. Frida, naturally surprised and upset, urged Louis and Mary to reconsider, asking Louis whether he was really willing to abandon his children.

Divorce was not a simple matter in Britain in the 1930s. It was not no fault—there had to be a reason given, usually adultery. The legal process took time. Socially, divorce was not acceptable to many people, including many of Louis's colleagues at Cambridge. Many thought his treatment of Frida had been cruel.

Louis, now joined by Mary, began to prepare for a new African expedition. Louis wanted to stop at Olduvai in order to learn more about what had gone wrong with their dating of Olduvai Man. They would then continue on to Kanam and Kanjera. They would be accompanied by three students and by Louis's critic Boswell, who had continued to raise questions about the dating of the fossils there.

Louis's parents, the retired missionaries, had strongly opposed his divorce. Louis and Mary decided that he would go on ahead to try to smooth things over, as well as dealing with Boswell's concerns. Mary was to join him six months later.

THE UNRAVELING

By November 1934, Louis and his team were back at Kanam. However, when he went to show his students where he had found the famous jaw, he could not find the right spot. Evidently, the iron stakes had disappeared, possibly stolen by local Luo people to make fishing harpoons or spears. Unfortunately, Louis had only one photo of the site, taken by a friend. (His own photos had been ruined by a camera problem.) Many of the gullies in the area looked similar, and Louis gradually realized that he would be unable to find the actual spot where the jaw had been found.

They went to Kanjera, where other skulls and tools had been found that seemed to support Louis's theories about early humanity. There, too, the iron stakes were missing, and again, photos were of no help. Leakey was chagrined and no doubt regretted his earlier failure to make a sketch map at the time of finding the fossils. Such a map might have given him enough clues to enable him to find the right place.

Boswell then arrived, expecting to begin examining the Kanam and Kanjera sites. First they went to Olduvai, where they studied the site where the problematic Reck Olduvai Man skull had been found. Finally Louis brought the increasingly impatient Boswell to Kanam and Kanjera. Boswell was dismayed when he realized that Louis had not been able to relocate the original sites with any sort of precision. The best they could do is find a few more bits of skull that looked similar to the earlier finds. Boswell angrily departed, feeling that he had wasted two months of time and effort on a wild goose chase.

Upon his return, Boswell was reluctant to say much about what had happened until Louis was back in the country and could defend himself. Nevertheless, word quickly spread through the scientific community. Colleagues who resented Leakey's arrogance and eye for publicity (or disapproved of his divorce) seemed happy with what appeared to be his downfall.

Still in Kenya, Louis seemed largely unaware of the uproar back home. He continued to report on new findings, including a new interest—ape fossils found on Rusinga Island in Lake Victoria. But in March 1936, Leakey received a letter from Haddon, his old backer and mentor, who was quite unhappy with him:

> The conference at Cambridge had to rely implicitly on your statements, and from what I hear there is much annoyance in view of recent developments. It seems to me that your future career depends largely upon the manner in which you face the criticisms. . . . if you want to secure the confidence of scientific men you must act bravely, and not shuffle. You may remember that more than once I have warned you not to be in too much of a hurry in your scientific work, as I feared that your zeal might overrun your discretion and I can only hope that it has not done so in this case.

Only then did Louis realize that Boswell must have reported in detail on the failure to corroborate the evidence at Kanam and Kanjera. He felt betrayed by Boswell because he thought they had agreed that nothing would be published until Louis's return.

MARY COMES INTO HER OWN

Meanwhile, while Louis and Boswell were dealing with the aftermath of the failure at Kanam and Kanjera, Mary had decided that she wanted to see African archaeology firsthand. The plan was for her to sail to Cape Town, South Africa, and view some prehistoric sites in the area. She would then take the train north to Rhodesia (now Zimbabwe) and fly the final leg to Tanganyika and meet Louis there. Everything worked fine until she arrived at the airport at Moshi . . . and no Louis was there. (His vehicle had gotten stuck in the rain-soaked roads.) When he finally arrived and saw Mary, he had good news. Despite the damage his reputation was still suffering, Louis had managed to get enough money to work again at Olduvai.

Mary would have to get used to the discomforts and occasional dangers of the African bush, but she was transfixed by the beauty of the countryside as they approached the site—herds of wildebeest and zebra, the occasional bellow of a rhino. As they drove down into the Serengeti Mary found, as she would record in *Disclosing the Past,* "In a few more miles, I was looking spellbound for the first time at a view that has since come to mean more to me than any other in the world." Louis eagerly showed Mary the many familiar landmarks, no doubt delighted at her response.

With camp reestablished at Olduvai and work underway, Mary quickly joined the effort to survey new fossil sites. In one part of Bed IV, Mary found her first human fossils (pieces of skull), with hand axes nearby. Excited, Louis started to excavate, but no more of the skull could be found.

Still, Mary's competence and energy began to win over Louis's colleagues. At first, some had disapproved of her because of her extramarital relationship with Louis, and others perhaps simply because she was a woman—females still being quite uncommon in field archaeology. Now, however, they could see that she was ready to take up any task, without asking for special favors.

Mary also learned about the constant struggle of Olduvai explorers to find enough drinking water in the dry season. Not having enough money to pay for gas to drive to faraway springs, they began to depend on the local ones—until they began to turn into wallows that attracted rhinos that rolled around in them. Soon, Mary observed, their soup, tea, or coffee all began to taste of rhino urine.

Another time a shower left water pooled in the hollow parts of their tent covers. They rushed to collect the freshwater, filling their glasses with it and gulping it down. Soon, they were violently sick. Unknown to them, their tents had been coated with heavy doses of arsenic-based insecticide.

Later, a native visitor, intrigued by their fossil hunting, offered to help. He also offered to guide them to a site where there were more "bones like stone." The place turned out to be Laetoli—the fossils were few, and the area's paleontological fame would lie in the future.

STONE AGE OASIS

The season at Olduvai had brought no great finds, though it was good experience for Mary and perhaps soothing to Louis after the Kanam/Kanjera uproar. Louis and Mary decided to close the operation early and spend the remaining six weeks worth of funds exploring more recent Stone Age sites in Tanganyika.

Louis had promised Mary that after they left Olduvai he would show her the rock paintings in a place called Kisese. Here the faces of the rocks were covered with a profusion of designs—lifelike antelope, elephants, rhinos, and the people themselves. For 10 days, Louis and Mary, aided by friendly Masai, explored the sites. There was also freshwater and fresh vegetables. After the hardships at Olduvai, "It was like a luxurious holiday," Mary would write in *Disclosing the Past*. Mary spent many hours making tracings of the paintings and hoped to return one day to study them in more detail.

An awkward time came when the couple returned to Nairobi and Louis went to stay with his parents. Mary took a room in a nearby hotel. It is not known what Louis told his parents about his plans for a life with Mary, but there was no meeting between them and her.

LOOSE ENDS

In fall 1935, Louis and Mary were back in England, their funds exhausted. Mary stayed with her mother in London. Cambridge had not renewed Louis's fellowship or offered any sort of work at all. Louis found a cheap cottage and moved his books, papers, and specimens there. A bit later Mary and her two dogs also moved in, making for a crowded home. By mid-20th century British standards the cottage was primitive—no electricity, not even running water. However, by African bush standards, it was almost luxurious.

The divorce with Frida would not be final for about a year. Meanwhile, Louis and Mary lived quietly and happily, though on the edge of poverty. Gradually, the financial situation began to improve a bit. After pleading to the Royal Society, it agreed to give him a grant of 100 pounds to finish writing up specimens he had collected. Writing also proved to be somewhat remunerative: He received royalty checks for *Adam's Ancestors* and an advance for a new book, *Kenya: Contrasts and Problems*. Some paid articles and lecture fees also helped.

Louis was also invited to give the prestigious Munro Lectures at Edinburgh University. Louis used this series of 10 lectures to present a systematic view of what was known about the prehistory of Africa. This presentation brought the big picture of African archaeology to the general public and would form the basis of a new book, *Stone Age Africa*. The lecture and book would encourage a new generation of students to look toward Africa for the study of human *evolution* and culture—students who in some cases would become important members of future Leakey expeditions.

Publishers seemed to be at least as interested in Leakey's life as in his work. In 1936, Louis received an advance for an autobiography, *White African*. The book was popular with both critics and ordinary readers, who were fascinated with tales of growing up with the Kikuyu, life in the African bush, and the hunt for tools and fossils.

DOCUMENTING THE KIKUYU

By fall 1936, Louis's financial situation had been relieved somewhat, but there was still the question of whether he would be able to return to Africa and continue his work in the field. The route would turn out to be indirect. Following the suggestion of an Oxford anthropologist, Louis wrote to the Rhodes Trust asking for funding for a study of the Kikuyu people and culture. He knew that he had unique qualifications for such a task. In his letter to the Trust he noted that

> I was born and bred among the Kikuyu tribe and speak their language better than I do English. I am a recognized member of one of the age groups (Mukanda) and also an initiated first grade elder . . . I feel that it is a duty which I owe to science and also to the Kikuyu people, to make use of my rather unusual position . . . and publish a detailed account of them . . .

Some of the trustees and their advisers were aware of the trouble Louis had gotten into over Olduvai man and the Kanam and Kanjeri fossils. In writing a letter of recommendation, Oxford anthropologist R. Coupland acknowledged Louis's weaknesses:

> He is an impulsive chap, & perhaps lacks the patience to be a first-rate scholar or scientist: & a good deal has been made recently of a blunder he is said to have made in prehistoric archaeology. But that doesn't, to my mind, make much difference. Even if he makes a slip or two (and who doesn't) the publication & lifelong knowledge of his Kikuyu is of first-rate importance. . . .

The Rhodes Trust apparently agreed with Coupland's views, for in October 1936 Louis received a grant of 500 pounds to study the Kikuyu for one year. There were some questions—notably, would Louis's close connections with the Kikuyu be enough for him to get the cooperation he would need from the tribe? Louis and Mary agreed that this project was the only chance they could see to get out of their cramped cottage and back to where anthropology and archaeology could be done.

Finally, in October, the divorce was settled, and Louis and Mary were free to marry. They did so on Christmas Eve, in a simple civil ceremony at the registry office in the town of Ware. Their best man, perhaps appropriately, was a Kikuyu—Peter, the son of Louis's old friend Chief Koinange, who was beginning graduate studies at Cambridge.

MEETING WITH THE ELDERS

Upon their arrival in Nairobi, Louis and Mary went to the village of Chief Koinange, who was an old and good friend of Louis and had also taken to Mary. Despite Louis's intimate ties with the Kikuyu, there had been decades of tension between whites and Kikuyu, stemming from the colonial policies that had forced many Kikuyu off their land and imposed an unfamiliar way of life on them. To the Kikuyu who had not grown up with him, Louis might be viewed as just another white man who wanted to take something and not necessarily give something in return.

Chief Koinange called a meeting of about 100 elders. As they sat in the shade of a sacred tree, Louis asked them for their cooperation. As recalled in *By the Evidence,* he said that his book was being written "so that the young people of future generations would really know and understand how the Kikuyu had lived." He promised that he would not do anything that would hurt the tribe. After about a week of discussion, the elders agreed to Louis's request and appointed nine senior elders to advise him.

Louis immediately set to work on what he decided would be not one book, but three volumes, a virtual encyclopedia of Kikuyu culture. It would include everything from how they built their huts to social organization and warfare, to myth and the use of medicinal plants. He painstakingly interviewed elders who had particular knowledge of a matter, then corroborated their statements by interviewing still other elders.

Mary was not idle during this time. She went to nearby Waterfall Cave and dug for prehistoric remains and artifacts, practicing her field skills with the aid of some of Louis's Kikuyu. Suddenly, however, Mary came down with a high fever. A local doctor diagnosed malaria and gave her a shot of quinine, but her fever only got worse. Fearing the worst, Louis drove Mary overnight to Nairobi Hospital. The doctors there found that Mary had double pneumonia (an infection in both lungs).

The doctor suggested that Mary's mother be summoned from England, for in a time before antibiotics the disease was almost always fatal. In the days of slow propeller planes, the journey to Kenya would take several legs over four days, and no one knew whether she would arrive in time.

The only treatment was intensive nursing and oxygen, and no staff was available. Louis became his wife's nurse, spending hour after hour at her bedside. In *By the Evidence,* Mary recalled that perhaps the most important thing she received from Louis during that time was that he was determined that "I should not give up: somehow he managed to convey this to me." Finally, after many days, Mary recovered.

The couple returned to work—Louis with the Kikuyu elders, and Mary tackling a new archaeological dig, at a place called Hyrax Hill, named for its profusion of the small rodentlike mammals. Mary and her crew found burial pits. The skeletons inside were primarily from young men, so Mary speculated that the deaths might have occurred in some sort of battle. On the other side of the hill were the remains of a Stone Age village, with a scattering of pottery and obsidian tools. All together, Hyrax Hill offered a glimpse of life in the late Stone Age *(Neolithic)* period, with sporadic habitation as late as a couple of hundred years ago.

Despite being rather recent, the Hyrax Hill site fascinated many local people, who had not realized how long people had been living in the area. Some visitors were moved to contribute financially, and Mary's work soon became self-supporting, making for one less burden on the Leakey's finances. The farmer who owned some adjacent land even bought Hyrax

Hill and donated it to the government. The site later became a national monument.

One visitor brought special news. Nellie Grant and her husband ran a large farm at Njoro, in the hills south of Hyrax Hill. When she returned home after visiting Mary's dig, Nellie began to look around the farm and soon found some beads and pottery in a cave behind the farm. Returning to Hyrax Hill, Nellie invited the Leakeys to come and see the cave. As soon as they began digging in the cave, the Leakeys hit pay dirt: a site where late Stone Age people had burned and buried their dead. Eventually, the Njoro River cave yielded dozens of skeletons and a trove of jewelry and even the remains of baskets and fabrics.

WARTIME SPY

As Louis's work continued, he realized there was no way he could finish his extensive study in only a year. Seeing no other options, he applied to the Rhodes Trust and received another 500 pound grant for the coming year. However, their long-term support was still in question. One promising area was the possibility that the Kenyan colonial government would establish a department of archaeology or antiquities and perhaps a museum. With his Kenyan background and archaeological experience, Louis might be the ideal candidate to head such an effort. However, the proposal was rejected, in part because by 1939 East Africa, like the rest of the British Empire, was worried about the likely prospect of war with Nazi Germany and the Italians, who had already invaded Ethiopia to the north.

The same war jitters eventually proved to be a source of new employment for Louis. The Kenyan authorities were increasingly worried that German or other foreign agents were stirring up unrest in the native community. Louis had a deep sympathy for the Kikuyu people and understood why they might be resentful and angry at the colonial government. Nevertheless, he believed that an outright rebellion would be disastrous for both the Kikuyu and the white settlers. Louis agreed that he would gather intelligence about possible subversive threats. He supplemented his existing network of Kikuyu people with a cover as a trader, enabling him to circulate throughout the countryside. The salary he received certainly helped with the Leakeys' expenses, but Louis's archaeological career was at a virtual standstill.

As 1940 progressed, the Nazis rolled through Europe while the Italians spread their influence from Ethiopia to Somalia and then into British

Somaliland. With bases on the Red Sea, there was danger that the Italians could capture Egypt and particularly the Suez Canal. If they succeeded, Britain would be cut off from India and its Asian possessions, with ships forced to sail all the way around the tip of Africa.

The British fought back by supplying Ethiopian guerrilla forces. Even as British agents moved through northern Kenya into Ethiopia, enemies could use the same route to infiltrate into the British colony to the south. For a time Louis was kept busy, using his knowledge of native languages and customs to interrogate suspected agents and insurgents. (He also sometimes used his trips to gather a crate or two of fossils!)

Louis also helped Kenya's Criminal Investigation Department monitor what it saw as domestic threats—Kikuyu political organizations that the government disbanded as a wartime precautionary measure. He pored through thousands of confiscated documents from the groups to gather evidence against their leaders, who had been arrested. In the case of one group, the Kikuyu Central Association, Louis determined that the documents did indicate that the group had intended to aid enemy forces. While Louis did not support the tactics of such radical organizations (he preferred moderate reformers), he believed that the government's heavy-handed measures were likely to only stir up more trouble in the long run.

ARCHAEOLOGY IN WARTIME

Meanwhile, Mary was free to pursue archaeology, and she continued her work. At a particularly rich site (a rock shelter about to be destroyed for railroad development), Mary and her crew unearthed, sorted, and labeled more than 75,000 stone tools, plus innumerable chips and shards. Unfortunately, while Mary was away, termites (the particularly voracious African kind) ate through all the labeled cardboard boxes, dumping all the tools back into a jumbled pile.

By spring 1940, Mary was pregnant with the Leakey's first child. She gave up further excavations to work at the Coryndon Museum in Nairobi. In January 1941, Louis was able to join her part time as an honorary (unpaid) curator. Their child, Jonathan Harry Erskine Leakey, had been born the previous November. The next two years continued the mix of Louis's wartime work and some archaeological digging (particularly by Mary). In *By the Evidence*, Mary records one big find at a place called Olorgesailie, about 40 miles (64 km) south of Nairobi, where "in an area of about fifty by sixty feet [15 by 18 meters] there were literally hundreds upon hundreds of perfect, very large hand axes and cleavers, as well as a few flakes and some bolas stones (round stone balls.)"

Tragedy struck the Leakeys when their second child, a daughter named Deborah, died from dysentery at the age of three. Both Mary and Louis were deeply affected by their loss, and little work was done for several months. Finally, though, they returned to Olorgesailie. Louis had a new idea: He believed that the presence of all the tools and fossils indicated what archaeologists call a living floor, a regularly used camp site where animals were periodically slaughtered, leading to the accumulation of hand axes and bones. Always searching for information about the hand axe culture, or Acheuleans, the excavation (supervised mainly by Mary) proceeded layer by layer, as though it were a later stone age camp or village.

Louis was always willing to exercise his vivid imagination, and he painted a mental picture of a group of skilled hunters who could systematically drive animals where they could be killed with clubs or stones. He based this picture in part on the presence of many large animals (such as giant pigs and huge baboons), all of which had smashed skulls and broken bones. Louis believed that the damage had been done by early humans using those large hand axes to get at the rich bone marrow.

Louis even had a theory about the bolas stones. He knew that some native people hunted with a weapon called a bola—three stone balls tied together and thrown to entangle the legs of the prey and bring it down. Louis concluded that early humans must have used a similar weapon. The sinews fastening the stones must have long ago disintegrated, leaving only the balls behind. In *By the Evidence*, Louis describes how "I personally tried an experiment with bolas on one occasion . . . but was forced to give up after I nearly killed myself."

While painting quite a romantic tableau of the life of distant human ancestors, later researchers have dashed cold water on Louis's theories. Geologists have concluded that the accumulation of tools and bones at Olorgesailie was not due to people camping there over many years, but the result of the objects being washed into ancient stream channels and piling up at the bottom. As for the stone balls, later experts on stone tools concluded that the round stones were actually shaped that way from their repeated use for hammering other stones to make tools. As they were held at different angles, the hammer stones would gradually be flattened and rounded.

THOUGHTS OF ANCIENT APES

During the war years, Louis's interest in even more distant human ancestors increased. He began to look toward the *Miocene* period, about 20 million years ago, where he hoped to find ancestors in the deep roots of the primate tree—ancestors of old world monkeys on the one hand and both

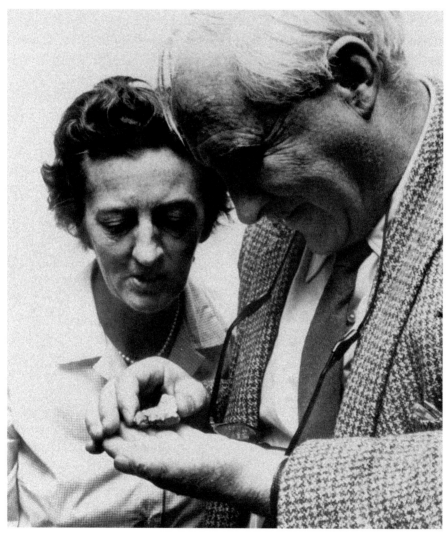

Mary Leakey's discovery of *Proconsul africanus* pushed back the fossil history of the common ancestors of humans and modern apes. At a news conference held March 22, 1962, in Washington, D.C., Louis and Mary Leakey look at a bone of a primate believed to be 14 million years old. *(AP Images)*

humans and the various great apes such as chimpanzees and gorillas on the other.

Back in 1909, a gold prospector in Kenya had discovered the jaw of an apelike creature. In the early 1930s, Louis's colleague Arthur Hopwood had joined him in exploring sites near Lake Victoria. Hopwood found three more specimens of the creature, which he assigned the name *Proconsul africanus*. (This was a joke: the name "Consul" was being used for certain circus chimpanzees, and "Proconsul" means "before Consul." *Proconsul* indeed is a remote ancestor of the modern chimp.

In 1942, while on leave from his wartime intelligence duties, Louis and Mary and a small party were exploring Rusinga Island in Lake Victoria, scouting areas for future fossil digging. Suddenly Louis saw a jaw jutting out of the rock face. It was from *Proconsul,* and it was the finest, most complete specimen of that species found to date. Following his typical inclination to see human characteristics as far back in time as possible, Louis insisted (in a letter quoted in *Ancestral Passions)* that "this specimen has many characters which seem to link it more with man than with the great apes." (Most other researchers did not agree, seeing *Proconsul* as being more likely a common ancestor of both great apes and the Old World monkeys.)

From Rusinga to Olduvai

By the end of 1944, the war was beginning to wind down—Germany, Italy, and Japan were no longer in a position to threaten British Africa, and Louis's services as a spy were now rarely needed. Louis therefore began to think about how he would be able to support his family and their work in the postwar period. With the bridges to Cambridge largely burnt by past controversy, the Leakeys' best chance seemed to be found in Kenyan institutions.

Both Louis and Mary had spent many hours as volunteers helping the Coryndon Museum. As honorary curator, Louis had not been paid, and they had even had to pay rent to use the curator's house, which was in considerable disrepair, infested with, among other things, fierce stinging ants that had swarmed over and nearly killed their son, Jonathan.

Louis began to complain more stridently about his treatment, and the museum trustees rather grudgingly awarded him a single honorarium payment of 150 pounds. Considering the many ways in which he had promoted the museum to visitors and how he had patiently answered hundreds of questions about archaeology, Louis thought this was little enough (the previous curator had received an annual salary six times greater).

Meanwhile Louis applied for a variety of positions and grants, including some in London and even Cambridge, though he seemed reluctant to consider leaving Kenya, where more exploration waited. Finally, the museum offered him a permanent position as curator at 750 pounds (about $2,125.00) a year. Louis accepted, though he complained to the trustees that they could have been more generous. It came just in time, because on December 19, 1944, their second son, Richard, was born.

THE PAN-AFRICAN CONGRESS

The end of the war and the easing of travel restrictions made it possible for Mary to make a visit to England for the first time in eight years. Mary's mother, Cecilia, was quite ill and had been pleading for Mary to come home so she could visit with her and her sons Jonathan and Richard. Unfortunately, they would only have a short time together: Cecilia died only two weeks after their arrival in April 1945. With most of the shipping being used for returning troops, it would be some time before they could obtain passage back to Africa.

While Mary settled her mother's affairs and visited relatives, Louis, back in Kenya, had to throw all his time and effort into the Pan-African Congress of Prehistory. Back in 1944 when he had proposed the idea, Louis had received enthusiastic support from colleagues in South Africa and even England.

Many felt the time for such a meeting had come. The true importance of Africa for the study of human origins was finally being recognized, thanks to a growing number of key fossils discoveries by Raymond Dart, Louis Leakey, and others. There were now at least three main areas of research.

Several early ape ancestors (going back perhaps 20 million years) had been found in East Africa, though their relationship to subsequent human development was controversial. (Louis tended to think of nearly all early fossil *hominins* as humanlike, while others were inclined to see them as ancestors of modern apes.) Louis's growing interest in Rusinga Island was related to the apparent abundance of early *primate* fossils.

Another group of species, the australopithecines, were even harder to disentangle from the human line. The australopithecines, living between about 4 and 2 million years ago, had some humanlike characteristics (such as upright *bipedal* posture and hands that could grip with some precision), even if it was unclear whether they were direct human ancestors. Raymond Dart's Taung baby was the most famous australopithecine discovery, but skulls, jaws, and other fragments had been found in South Africa.

The search for direct human ancestors associated with stone tools such as hand axes had been a strong interest of Louis (and later Mary) since the days of the Kanam and Kanjeri diggings. Many age estimates were gradually

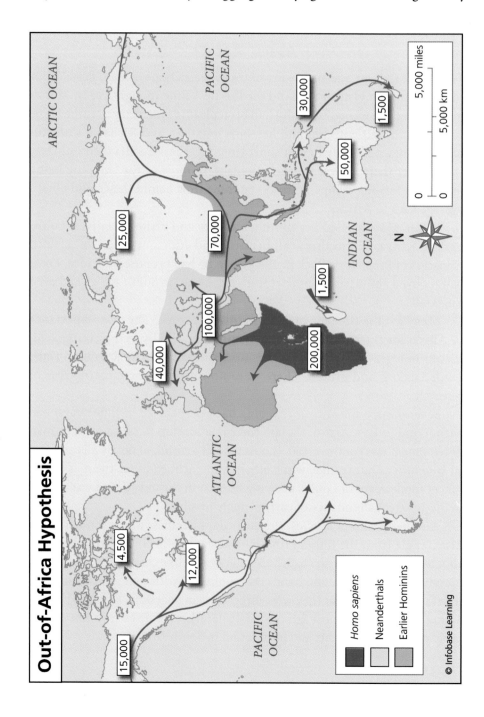

Out-of-Africa Hypothesis

Homo sapiens
Neanderthals
Earlier Hominins

© Infobase Learning

Distribution of Hominin Species

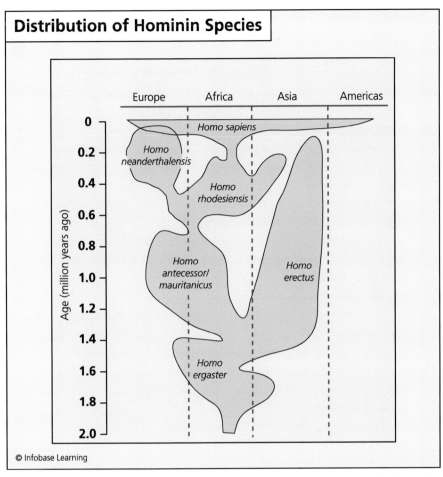

A graph that shows how various species of humans (hominins) spread geographically during the past 2 million years

being pushed back into the past, but Louis's failure to properly fix the location of his earlier finds had taken important fossils off the table.

Besides wanting the upcoming conference to give a boost to new fossil-hunting projects (particularly in East Africa), Louis also hoped that such a serious and thoughtful meeting would help restore his personal reputation. The failures at Kanam and Kanjera had left Louis with a reputation for

(continues on page 52)

(opposite page) According to the *Out-of-Africa hypothesis,* successive waves of human ancestors spread from Africa into Europe and Asia. Modern humans *(Homo sapiens)* are simply the latest such wave, and the only one to reach the Americas.

TERMINOLOGY, OR CLIMBING AROUND THE FAMILY TREE

To make sense of the discoveries of the Leakeys and their friends and rivals, it is necessary to know how biologists classify creatures (including humans and their near relatives).

The fundamental unit is the species. There are a number of ways to define this term, but a modern one relies on genetics. A species is a group of animals that share a common gene pool and are able to mate to mix and match their genes. In an evolutionary tree, the species are like the buds at the end of the smallest branches.

The next category is the genus (plural genera). A genus is a group of species that have a *common ancestor* (that is, in the family tree they branched off from some previous species). In tree terms a genus might look like a little branch with twigs.

The next level up is the family, to which one applies the same principle: A family would describe the group of genera that have the same common ancestor. After that, moving toward the trunk and roots of the tree, one has order, class, phylum, and kingdom. (Recently, two categories have been inserted: tribe between family and genus, and super family between family and order.)

It has long been agreed that humans belong to the order mammals and the class primates. But how are the various kinds of primates related to one another and to humans? Until the 1980s (that is, throughout Louis Leakey's career), there was a simple split between humans (hominoids) and apes (anthropoids). Thus, when a paleontologist during most of the 20th century said she had found a hominid fossil, she meant something on the human line of evolution after humans split off from the ancestors of chimpanzees and the other apes.

Now, however, it is known that the chimps and gorillas are more closely related to humans than are orangutans. In other words, the

(opposite page) A time line that shows the approximate duration of humans, human ancestors, and related species; according to the latest genetic research, the earliest human ancestors and chimpanzees parted ways about 5 million years ago.

common ancestor of chimps and gorillas (believed to have lived some-where between 5 and 7 million years ago) is later than the common ances-tor of humans, chimps/gorillas, *and* orangutans (that is, all the great apes).

(continues)

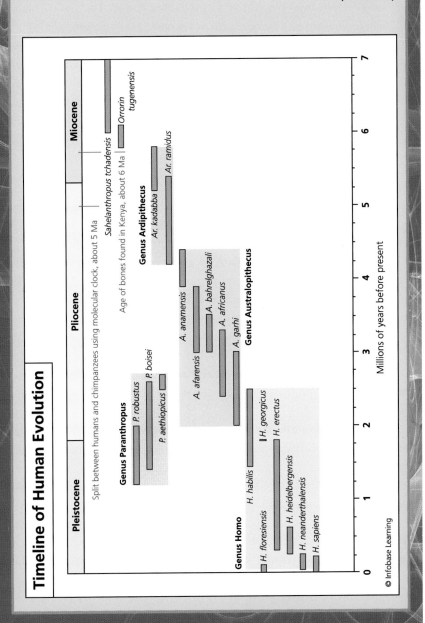

Timeline of Human Evolution

© Infobase Learning

(continued)

To distinguish the group of species that includes humans (and those species that are direct ancestors of modern humans) from the evolutionary line that became chimps and gorillas, humans and their direct ancestors have recently been grouped into a tribe called homini. Thus, now a hominin fossil might be a *Homo erectus* or a modern *Homo sapiens*.

What is confusing is that some people still use hominid to refer to what is now called hominin. In this book, the quoted terms are not changed, but hominin is used in the main text to refer to the human species and direct ancestors. It is safe enough for our purposes to consider the two terms equivalent.

(continued from page 49)
slipshod, unreliable work. Meanwhile, his willingness to play the media (giving interviews and articles to popular newspapers) and give numerous public lectures seemed distasteful to quieter, more circumspect colleagues.

On January 14, 1947, the Pan-African Congress opened with an impressive ceremony. Sixty scientists representing 26 countries attended. Papers and heated debates about Miocene apes and Stone Age toolmakers were interspersed with festive dinners and cocktail parties.

British archaeologist J. Desmond Clark (1916–2002) recalled in *A History of African Archaeology* that "When I arrived in Africa [in 1938], there were only two or three professional archaeologists in the whole of the continent south of the Sahara. [We] were separated by hundreds of miles and met only on rare occasions."

The Congress not only allowed archaeologists and anthropologists scattered across the continent to meet and compare notes, it also brought them together with practitioners of the related sciences necessary for a more comprehensive understanding of the prehistoric world. This included paleontologists, anatomists, and geologists.

As a result of Louis's own presentations, many scientists saw how extensively he had studied all aspects of African prehistory and left with a considerably higher regard for his work. At the same time, Mary Leakey emerged as a full-fledged archaeologist in her own right, as Louis described the significance of her work at Hyrax Hill, the Njoro River Cave, and Olorgesailie. A party from the conference got to see the Hyrax Hill site in person, noting the careful way Mary had excavated the site so that the relationship of the bones and stones to each other and to the archaeological *horizon* was preserved.

Louis also made or strengthened personal contacts that would be very important in aiding his future work. One of these was Wilfrid Le Gros Clark (1895–1971), a leading specialist in comparative anatomy who he first met in the 1930s. While Louis had a good eye for anatomical features and their significance, he sometimes misidentified features and would benefit by having a more careful and systematic anatomist on hand.

SEARCHING FOR APES IN RUSINGA

Just as the search for the more immediate human ancestors seemed to be pushing back in time from hundreds of thousands to millions of years, there was a growing interest in when and how humans and apes parted company. (Put another way, scientists were interested in finding the last common ancestor of humans and modern apes such as chimpanzees.)

At the Congress, Louis had received from Le Gros Clark a promise to help find funding for an expedition to Rusinga Island to follow up on the promising fossil beds Louis had spied there. Meanwhile, a previously unknown American named Wendell Phillips had also surfaced at the Congress. He had a bold plan for a huge expedition to both East and South Africa in order to find the key answers to human evolution.

Upon investigation it turned out that Phillips was not a scientist, but an energetic entrepreneur—and he had the backing of the University of California, Berkeley. Evidently he was quite successful in mobilizing resources: In a letter to Louis only three months after the Congress, Phillips reported that he had obtained $150,000 in funding, 10 vehicles, an airplane, plenty of fuel, ample other gear, and round-trip airfare for 20 scientists!

A little later, Louis had gained a rather more modest commitment—about 1,750 pounds and contributions from various companies of gasoline, tents, and a single airline ticket. By summer 1947, the irrepressible Phillips had amassed commitments of half a million dollars, more vehicles, a motorboat, and even the promise of the loan of a navy ship courtesy of U.S. admiral Chester Nimitz.

Phillips's plans then began to run out of steam, with arguments over whether to head first to East Africa or South Africa. The date was pushed back to spring 1948, giving Louis a window of opportunity to get on the (hopefully fossil-rich) ground ahead of the American juggernaut.

THE SCOUTING EXPEDITION

Louis and Mary headed out across Lake Victoria to Rusinga Island on a rented motor launch. They already knew about the rich fossil beds laid down under volcanic ash—back in 1942 Louis had found a jaw of *Proconsul* there. Returning to the spot, Louis now found a canine tooth from the primitive ape, and the team also excavated the skeleton of an ancient species of rhino. Making a brief venture to a nearby part of the mainland called Songhor, Louis also revisited an earlier site, finding the jaw fragment matching a tooth he had found back in 1932. Later, these fragments would be attributed to another early ape species, *Proconsul major.*

Altogether Louis, Mary, and their team found 64 fragments of the jaws and teeth of Miocene apes, as well as many other animals from that same period. The latter finds were important because researchers would be able to use them to reconstruct a picture of the environment in which these early primates lived. All together, the study of the "ancestors of human ancestors" had been pushed back to a new level, and the Leakey stock had also risen in the eyes of their backers.

Louis remained ambivalent toward Phillips and his plans. He did not want to appear selfish, but he did not want them tromping through Olduvai, Rusinga, or other areas that he viewed as his long-term projects. Finally, he and Phillips agreed that the latter could go to the virtually unexplored western side of Lake Rudolf (later called Lake Turkana). Writing to Le Gros Clark, Louis told him that Phillips would submit any significant hominid finds to him for analysis, but he also suggested that the Phillips expedition would likely fail. The American team had little knowledge of Africa or the particular area they would be searching. Louis also believed that the very size and complexity of Phillips's team would make it unwieldy.

The news media, having gotten word of Phillips's plans, portrayed the whole affair as a great race between Phillips and his Americans and the Kenyan-British Leakeys. Perhaps as a result of this sense of competition, British aid started to come to Louis. Even Percy Boswell, who had blasted Louis over the errors at Kanam and Kanjera, offered to help him get more money from the Royal Society. A promising source of private funding came from Charles Boise, a wealthy London businessman who believed that research into the ancient Miocene primates should be seen as a British enterprise. Boise soon provided a check for 1,000 pounds and the Kenyan government provided 1,500 pounds—enough to fund the next expedition to Rusinga.

Louis flew to England to confer with Le Gros Clark on how to handle the anatomical studies of the early primates, while also attending a geological congress. However, he soon had to rush to Kenya to his parents' home. His father had died in 1940, and now his mother was dying. The expedition would begin on a somber note.

The American expedition, headed by the geologist Basil Cooke, visited with Louis at the Coryndon Museum. After a polite if cool meeting, the Americans spent the summer and fall exploring western Lake Rudolf. They made a modest haul of a partial lower jaw and one tooth from a Miocene ape and a few less significant finds. The only really sour note came when Phillips arrived with a film crew, having issued a report on their fossil finds that described Louis as a member of his expedition. Understandably, this enraged the volatile Louis.

PROCONSUL

That summer Louis and Mary returned to Rusinga, their arrival delayed by Louis having a painful gall bladder attack. In *By the Evidence,* Louis would recall that "For some time we had both had a hunch—if that is the word for it—that something very important was near at hand. The problem was to locate it."

While Louis worked to excavate a crocodile skull, Mary went off to explore a nearby weathered rock face. She began to see some promising bone fragments and then suddenly a tooth was glinting from the rock. In *Disclosing the Past,* Mary recalls how the next moment "I was shouting for Louis as loud as I could and he was coming, running."

Giddy with excitement but working carefully, Louis and Mary began to brush away the earth. What had been a tooth soon became a jaw and then, as recorded in *By the Evidence,* "The greater part of a skull became visible." By the time they were finished, they had both jaws (with all their teeth) and much of the skull, including parts of the face. In *Disclosing the Past,* Mary would write:

> This was a wildly exciting find which would delight human paleontologists all over the world, for the size and shape of a hominid skull of this age, so vital to evolutionary studies, could hitherto only be guessed at. Ours were the first eyes ever to see a *Proconsul* face.

Back in camp came the painstaking process of gluing together the many small fragments that accompanied the major fossils of the skull. As more details emerged, Louis became increasingly convinced that this *Proconsul* was actually quite humanlike, more so than the later australopithecines.

News of the remarkably complete *Proconsul* find quickly spread through the paleontological community, where it was met with praise and enthusiasm. The actual specimen, fragile and small enough to fit in a cotton-lined biscuit tin, was carried on Mary's lap through the long trip back to London in late October 1948. When Mary stepped off the plane at London's Heathrow Airport, a crowd of reporters from newspapers, radio, and the newest media—television—awaited her.

To most of the media (and indeed the world), Leakey meant Louis Leakey. It took the press awhile to catch up with the fact that it was Mary who had first spotted the *Proconsul* and that it was she who had done much of the work of piecing together and analyzing the skull. At this time, the presence of women was still rare in the fields of archaeology and paleontology, which remained old boys' networks.

Meanwhile it was Le Gros Clark, the master anatomist, who hosted the skull in his lab, carefully measuring each feature and analyzing such factors as the slope of the forehead, the contours of the face, and the structure of the teeth. What did they say about the creature's brain capacity, what it ate, or its way of life?

As noted earlier, Louis had an initial impression that this *Proconsul* was humanlike. By this, he did not mean that it was a direct human ancestor. (Even with his proclivity for seeing a great antiquity for *Homo sapiens,* Louis knew that the approximately 20-million-year-old *Proconsul* could not be a direct human ancestor.) Rather, he thought that the line eventually leading to humanity might have diverged from that resulting in the modern apes somewhere upstream in time just before *Proconsul.* That would make *Proconsul,* with its lack of forehead slope and of the brow ridges associated with modern apes, an early step along the road to humanity.

At a press conference, Le Gros Clark and Mary Leakey tried to answer a barrage of questions about *Proconsul.* In the popular mind at least, there had been much talk for decades about the so-called *missing link*—a species that would presumably have both apelike and human features, illustrating the evolution that would eventually result in true humans. The two scientists tried to explain that their conclusions were only tentative at this point and that while *Proconsul* was a key fossil in primate evolution, its relationship to human evolution was necessarily remote and indirect. (Today, *Proconsul* is placed in the evolutionary tree not where humans and modern apes split, but much earlier, when the great apes and the monkeys parted company.)

Wherever this *Proconsul* find belonged in the evolutionary tree, it proved to be a great aid to Louis in raising funds to sustain further research into primate evolution. In addition to another grant from the Kenyan government, Charles Boise came through with money for Louis to buy a 42-foot (13 m) cabin cruiser that he christened the *Miocene Lady*. This ship made it easy for the Leakeys to go back and forth across Lake Victoria to Rusinga Island or other places of interest on the shore.

Aided by their new boat, the Leakey team continued its work at Rusinga in the early 1950s. Louis, having run into so much trouble by mistaking the geological context of Olduvai Man, had resolved to always have at least one geologist accompany his expeditions. Once, the geologist Thomas Whitworth was making a survey when he found a hole virtually crammed with fossils. Among them were more *Proconsul* parts, including not only a partial skull and jaws but also the arm, hand, and foot—the latter going a long way toward giving science a complete skeleton of the ancestral ape.

A TANGLED WEB

Amid all the celebration over the *Proconsul* find and for future work at Rusinga, Louis would soon have to deal with an old problem. He would again be called upon to work with the courts and police.

Following World War II, Britain, now eclipsed by the power of the United States and the USSR, was being forced to loosen the bonds connecting it to a worldwide empire it could no longer afford. At the same time, in the Caribbean, Asia, and particularly Africa, native peoples had increasingly, begun to organize movements for self-rule or independence. (The biggest remaining colony, India, had achieved independence in 1948.)

In Kenya, the British Colonial Office began to advocate for a multiracial government that would give equal shares of power to the white settlers, the black majority, and the considerable population of Asian immigrants. The basic idea was to give the blacks some political outlet without threatening the economic and property interests of the white farmers who controlled the rich coffee and tea plantations, dairy farms, and other enterprises.

The white settlers rejected even this moderate suggestion. Instead, they passed laws that ensured they would control the legislature and all other important institutions. Black Africans were restricted from property ownership in fertile highlands, forcing them to crowd in the poorest land. Segregation and apartheid laws (such as requiring the carrying of internal passports) similar to those being enacted in South Africa understandably led to a simmering resentment among Kenyan natives. By 1949, Louis had begun to warn the authorities of the secret ceremonies being held by the most militant group, the Mau Mau.

The Kikuyu among whom Louis had grown up had been the worst victims of greedy and shortsighted policies. In the book *African Journeys* by Fenner Brockway, Senior Chief Koinange (Louis's old friend) describes the feelings of many of his people:

> When someone steals your ox, it is killed and roasted and eaten. One can forget. When someone steals your land, especially if nearby, one can never forget. It is always there, its trees which were dear friends, its little streams. It is a bitter presence.

CAUGHT IN A DILEMMA

Louis always spoke of his close ties to the Kikuyu people and his experiences gave him an understanding of their language and way of life that was available to few whites. In his 1936 book *Kenya: Contrasts and Problems,* Louis had argued that Kenya could "never really be a white man's country" and urged the British and other Europeans to "work towards co-operation (with the Africans) instead of domination." These views were not popular with the white settlers, who considered him to be much too closely aligned with the natives and a traitor to white interests.

On the other hand, as many Kikuyu became increasingly angry and militant, white liberal reformists such as Louis were being viewed with suspicion. After all, during the war, Louis had worked with intelligence and police forces that rounded up blacks who were considered to be potential troublemakers—often based upon flimsy suspicions. Now, in the 1950s, Louis was involved in advising whites how to combat the Mau Mau insurgency, and the Mau Mau retaliated by threatening him with death and posting a reward for his head. The Leakeys started carrying guns wherever they went and were accompanied by police guards.

The Mau Mau killed chiefs who were appointed by or who cooperated with the white government, ambushed farmers, and conducted other forms of terrorism. In October 1952, a spate of such killings led to a government sweep that resulted in the arrest of 82 nationalist leaders, including the most popular one of all, Jomo Kenyatta.

Kenyatta was charged with being a Mau Mau leader, with his political group the Kenya African Union (KAU) being simply a front for the radical group. There was little actual evidence for the charges, and later historians would condemn the ensuing trial as being thoroughly corrupt, with the judge conferring with the prosecutor behind closed doors and the testimony of government witnesses bought and paid for.

Louis was asked to be the court translator for Kikuyu documents and testimony. Although he was certainly a foremost expert on the Kikuyu, he had also been a government agent since the 1940s and was participating actively in the government's investigation leading up to the trial. By any account, Louis could not be considered impartial.

Louis's role in the trial of Jomo Kenyatta was complicated by the long relationship between the men. Kenyatta's wife, Grace Wahu, had been educated by Louis's mother at the mission. Later, Louis and Kenyatta had quarreled over the latter's increasingly radical political views. The two had even argued over Kikuyu customs and anthropology.

Louis's translations during the trial were attacked as biased and unacceptable to the defense, and he was eventually forced to withdraw. However, he was later asked to return and translate KAU documents, looking for references to a connection with the Mau Mau. Louis found only vague references, but the judge Ramsley Thacker convicted Kenyatta and sentenced him, along with five other men, to sentences of seven years at hard labor. Kenyatta's house and farm were also confiscated.

Outright war erupted as armed Mau Mau took to the forest and fought a guerrilla campaign against British troops and their native recruits. During this three-year period, called the Kenya Emergency, Louis continued to work his intelligence contacts to try to track down Mau Mau leaders. (One time, he even tried to enlist his sister Julia, who was working among the Kikuyu as a missionary. Julia refused to betray what she regarded as her Kikuyu friends.) Louis also wrote about the Mau Mau crisis, including a series of newspaper articles and a book, *Defeating Mau Mau*. In his writings, he tried to use his knowledge of the Kikuyu to develop a sort of psychological warfare against the insurgents.

Louis did continue his paleontological work alongside what could be called counterinsurgency operations. Although he was frequently threatened by the militants, he was never actually physically attacked, let along injured. (The closest he came to injury was when he and Mary discovered their car had been sabotaged by a loose bolt, which might have resulted in a fatal accident.)

Gradually, the government gained the upper hand against the Mau Mau and a sort of uneasy peace returned to Kenya. Kenyatta was released from prison to become the first president of an independent Kenya in 1964.

SEARCHING FOR "OUR MAN"

Since Louis's involvement in the turmoil of Kenya's Emergency made it more difficult for him to devote full attention to fossil hunting and research, Mary took on an increasing amount of the workload. Both Leakeys agreed to focus on Olduvai with its seemingly inexhaustible fossil deposits. Their goal was Louis's long-held dream: Find a fossil that would prove that distinctly human features developed early in hominin evolution—several million years ago at least. Their search for fossils indisputably linked to the earliest stone tools, revealing the nature of those first toolmakers, was a related interest. The Leakeys had begun to refer to this hypothetical but highly desired fossil as "Our Man."

In 1952, Louis and Mary focused on Bed II, the second-oldest Olduvai layer. This was the lowest layer where stone hand axes had been found. It was logical that their makers would eventually be found there as well. The Leakeys had an interesting system for naming the various gorges and outcroppings at Olduvai. The first part of the name was that of the member of the team who had first found and explored the feature. The second part consisted of the name of the feature—usually a *korongo* (gully). Thus, the places where they were now digging were referred to as BK (Peter Bell Korongo) and SHK (Sam Howard Korongo).

BK turned out to have hundreds of stone tools and flakes together with a huge pile of fossil bones from animals such as giant pigs, buffalo, and antelopes. There were no human fossils, but Louis believed he had figured out the significance of what had been found. In a letter quoted in *Ancestral Passions,* Louis reported that:

> We have not yet got the man, but I think we have found a most likely place to get him. . . . We found a 'slaughter house' . . . where he drove hundreds of animals into a sticky bog of clay and then, when they were bogged down, killed and cut them up.

As earlier with Olorgesailie, other researchers would dispute this interpretation of the findings. The tools and bones being together might be the result of their being piled up by a stream, rather than being the remains of a single slaughterhouse. The hominins may not have actually camped at that site—but perhaps some of their remains might be found nearby.

Louis's imagination, so useful for visualizing possible areas of research, could run away with him sometimes. One example was his piecing together a fossil of a milk molar (part of a child's first set of teeth). Because it was so large, yet from a child, Louis suggested that the child might have been from a species of giants, massive people much larger than modern humans. (Later, it was determined that the tooth was from an australopithecine, not a *Homo*.)

FINDING "ZINJ"

By 1959, the Leakeys, not finding much in Bed II of Olduvai, had decided to dig down into the lowest layer, Bed I, where they were encouraged by the finding of a hominin molar. Of course, they wanted to continue the excavation to see if there was more of the fossil around. However, the money allocated for the season was close to running out, so Louis had to dash off to Nairobi to get a loan against his future contributions.

What happened next is a perfect illustration of how big a role luck can play in the search for significant human fossils. First, Louis agreed to delay

A plaque marks the spot where *Australopithecus boisei* (later named *Paranthropus boisei*) was found by Many Leakey in 1959—note the rugged surrounding terrain with its layers of sediment and exposed rock. (*GGS, 2009, used under license from Shutterstock.inc.*)

resumption of the digging so two friends who were producing a television show called "On Safari" could bring in their cameraman to film the proceedings. Meanwhile, Louis and Mary scouted out some sites for future exploration.

On the morning of July 17, 1959, Louis was not feeling well—he had a low-grade fever suggesting flu. Mary insisted that he stay in camp while she went out to explore new sites. A bit worried about Louis, Mary decided not to take the long trip she had planned. Instead, she decided to take a look at a nearby outcropping called FLK (for Frida Leakey's Korongo). (Back in 1931 Louis had found his first Olduvai stone tools in FLK, but they had not really investigated it further.)

Slowly crawling up the slope, Mary scanned carefully for anything that might be significant—tools, shards, bits of bone, perhaps a tooth . . . As she worked in the hot glare of the noontime Sun, she found a sliver of bone. If that was all it was, it would not be very significant. However, as narrated in *Disclosing the Past,* Mary noticed that the bone "was not lying loose on the surface but projecting from beneath. It seemed to be part of a skull. . . . It had a hominid look, but the bones seemed enormously thick—too thick, surely."

As she began to brush away the earth, it soon became evident that it was indeed a hominin skull. It seemed to be in situ—no evidence of it having drifted from elsewhere. It had the possibility of being quite complete.

Driving quite recklessly back to camp, Mary burst in on Louis, who lay groggy from fever. As recounted in the article "Finding the World's Earliest Man," Mary shouted, "I've got him! I've got him! I've got him!" "Got what?" asked Louis. "Are you hurt?" "Him, the man! Our man," she replied. "The one we've been looking for. Come quick. I've found his teeth!"

As Louis recalled in a later National Geographic film, "I became magically well in a matter of moments." In "Finding the World's Earliest Man," Louis said he turned to look at Mary

> . . . and we almost cried with sheer joy, each seized by the terrific emotion that comes rarely in life. After all our hoping and hardship and sacrifice, at last we had reached our goal—we had discovered the world's earliest known human.

"DEAR BOY, WHAT ARE YOU?"

But how human was it, actually? It soon became clear from the teeth that they were looking at some variety of *Australopithecus.* This was a real prob-

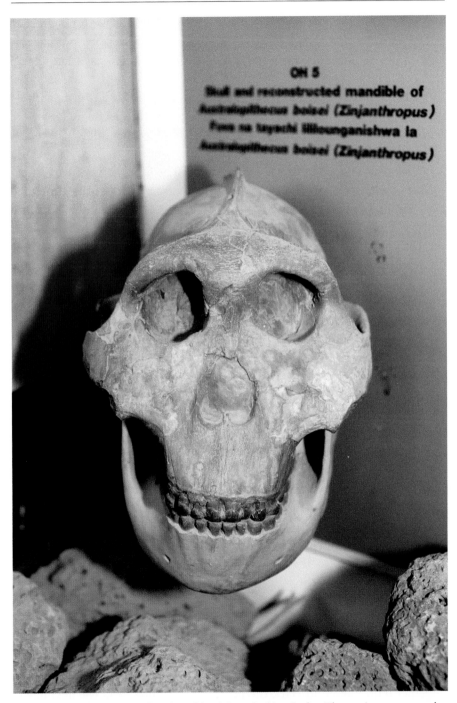

OH 5
Skull and reconstructed mandible of
Australopithecus boisei (Zinjanthropus)
Fuvu na tayachi lililounganishwa la
Australopithecus boisei (Zinjanthropus)

A skull of *Zinjanthropus boisei* found in Olduvai Gorge by Mary Leakey. The species was renamed twice; first to *Australopithecus boisei* and later to *Paranthropus boisei*. (*Arco Images GmbH/Alamy*) lem for Louis, because in his view australopithecines were not human ancestors, but a side branch in the evolutionary tree. Nevertheless, as he saw how complete the skull was likely to be, he knew that it was an important find in the overall scheme of prehistory.

This time, Louis would make sure that no lost markers or misidentified photos would destroy the value of the find as an in situ specimen. He waited until a photographer could come and extensively document the fossil and its surroundings.

Two ideas seemed to war in Louis's mind: The fossil had been accompanied by some stone tools. Louis, like many researchers of the time, had excluded the idea that *Australopithecus* could be a toolmaker, due to its limited brain capacity. Perhaps, then, this fossil with australopithecine-type teeth might be something else . . . a new, primitive version of *Homo* perhaps?

Only a day or so later, after examining teeth, jaws, and skull, Louis concluded that what they were looking at was a species that still had strong affinities with *Australopithecus* but had already branched off in a different direction—toward *Homo*. Meanwhile, Mary began to piece together about 400 pieces of the skull of what both Leakeys had taken to calling "Dear Boy." The result was a skull that was mostly complete, except for the lower jaw.

As the skull was introduced to the world, its proper place among hominin species became a topic for much debate. The more Louis looked at the find, the more differences he saw from the standard australopithecine type— he enumerated 20 differences in all. Acknowledging that the new fossil had broad resemblances to *Australopithecus,* he agreed that it should be included in the subfamily (grouping of genera) Australopithecinae. However, moving one level down in the hierarchy, Louis insisted that the new find belonged to a new genus. He thus proposed the name *Zinjanthropus boisei.* (*Zinjanthropus* means "human" from the Zinj region [of the coast of East Africa]: *boisei* honored Charles Boise, the Leakey's longtime financial backer.)

The publication of the official report on the fossil was delayed by a printers' strike. Meanwhile, Louis started to show "Zinj" to certain colleagues. On their way to the Fourth Pan-African Congress on Prehistory in Leopoldville in the Belgian Congo (now Kinshasha, Zaire), Louis and Mary stopped in South Africa and met the anatomist Phillip Tobias (1925–   ). Opening a little locked wooden box in their hotel room, they showed "Zinj" to Tobias. Together with Raymond Dart, the Leakeys and Tobias went the next day to the museum in Witwatersrand to compare "Zinj" to the extensive collection of australopithecines housed there.

Louis Leakey measures a prehistoric skull found in the Olduvai Gorge in 1960. *(AP Images)*

"Zinj" and the australopithecines had the same overall look—large teeth and powerful jaws, a rather small braincase. However "Zinj" was "heftier"— seemingly more solidly built—than the specimens in Dart's collection. "Zinj" also had a thick *sagittal crest.* The shape of the eyebrow ridges and the amount of protrusion of the face also differed somewhat. But did all of this add up to making "Zinj" a new species or even a new genus? One argument against that was the similarity between "Zinj" and the group of *robust* australopithecines that Robert Broom (1866–1951) had called *Paranthropus* (meaning "alongside man"). These fossils were also robust and had the sagittal crest. Louis, however, insisted that there were significant differences between "Zinj" and *Paranthropus.*

Zinjanthropus Boisei Skull

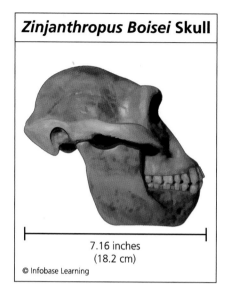

7.16 inches
(18.2 cm)

© Infobase Learning

An artist's depiction of the skull of *Zinjanthropus boisei*, showing its structure from the side

The opinion of most specialists (including Le Gros Clark) however, was against Louis's view. Undeterred, Louis mounted the podium at the Fourth Congress and announced that he was calling Mary's find *Zinjanthropus boisei*. He went on to say that Zinj, though similar to the australopithecines and still primitive, was clearly on the way to being human.

Later, researchers took turns coming up to the table where "Zinj" was laid out for inspection. The usual reaction of the viewers was to praise the Leakeys for their find but to question the chosen name. Most felt that "Zinj" was a robust australopithecine. Whimsically, as recounted in *Ancestral Passions,* Dart turned to Louis and said, "I can't help wondering what would have happened if Mrs. Ples [a nickname for one of the robust australopithecines] had met Dear Boy ("Zinj") on a dark night?" The group exploded with laughter, but they got the point: In order to mate successfully, "Zinj" and the robust australopithecine would have had to belong at least to the same genus, if not the same species.

Following the meeting, Louis and "Zinj" went on tour, first to London, and then to the United States, where he lectured 66 times at 17 universities in the space of a single month. Louis's story made for good press—decades of effort by a dedicated scientific couple finally resulting in the discovery of a key link to human evolution. A *National Geographic* feature article in September 1960 had the title "Finding the World's Earliest Man." Louis kept insisting "Zinj" was more than 600,000 years old. However, a new way of dating the volcanic ash in which "Zinj" was found came up with a different age: 1.75 million years. Whatever "Zinj" was, he was very old indeed.

DINNER WITH THE LEAKEYS

With the Coryndon Museum becoming an internationally famous paleo-anthropological and archaeological center, a steady stream of scientists came to visit both the fossil collections and the Leakeys themselves. Visiting the Leakey house was a complete adventure in itself. For one thing, there were the animals: Mary's Dalmatians, scurrying hyraxes, duikers (tiny antelopes), monkeys, an eagle owl (whose nest was atop a cupboard), and an assortment of snakes, many poisonous. Visitors learned that they were expected to share their plate and even their drink with any hyrax that took an interest in it. As for the backyard, it was more like a village, filled with little cinderblock huts housing the African workers and their families.

The seeming pandemonium of daily life at the Leakeys' house was in contrast to the curious formality of dinner. Louis provided the bread (he was a rather slapdash cook, but his baking became famous) and carved the meat. The cuisine partook more of London (roast beef with potatoes, for example) than of Africa.

It was conversation that was the real feast at the Leakey table. Certainly, Louis led discussions on archaeological and anthropological issues with his scientific visitors, but there were discussions about almost any other topic of interest, not to mention Louis's endless supply of stories about his adventures in bush and camp.

By contrast, Mary was more reticent, taking little part in the conversation. The boys (Jonathan and Richard) also felt restrained by the curiously formal relationship between father and sons. (Richard and Jonathan also came to greatly dislike each other and would address each other only indirectly.)

MARY DIGS IN

The speaking tours and popular magazine articles made Leakey a household word in Britain and the United States. Funds began to pour in, particularly from the National Geographic Society, which began its long-term funding of the Leakey's work. As the 1960s began, Louis's international activities and his position as curator of the Coryndon Museum meant that he could only visit Olduvai on the weekend or during vacation. He made Mary the director of the ongoing work at Olduvai.

Mary made a striking if rather eccentric picture as the director of all things Olduvai. As she strode around giving precise and emphatic instructions to the diggers, sorters, and camp crew, she invariably had a cigarette in hand and was always surrounded by her Dalmatian dogs. (Anyone caught mistreating one of her dogs was sure to receive a tongue-lashing.)

Unlike Louis, Mary kept a strict social distance from the Kamba native workers. In the evening, she would sit at her little table eating the dinner provided by her cook. The native workers would eat around their own camp-

A drawing of an early human found by Louis Leakey *(Peter V. Bianchi/National Geographic/Getty Images)*

In 1965, Mary Leakey and her crew sift through a dry wash at Olduvai Gorge, looking for bits of skull. *(Melville B. Grosvenor/National Geographic/Getty Images)*

fire. Sometimes, they would share stories or complaints about Mary, who they referred to as a "kali mzungu" or "prickly white" woman. The ways of the Leakey family seemed quite puzzling to them. As recalled by Kimoya Kimeu in *Ancestral Passions*:

> If a Kamba lady makes a mistake, the husband can beat her. But Mary was doing the opposite. If Louis makes a mistake, she almost beats Louis. So when we talk about Mary, we laugh very much.

They might laugh in the evening, but by day they did what Mary told them to do—and quietly. One time, as the workers began to dig a trench, they started to sing a traditional garden-digging song. Mary immediately told them that this was no garden and to stop singing immediately. Some of the workers grew tired of such a restrictive atmosphere and left the camp.

KAMOYA KIMEU: MASTER FOSSIL FINDER

Kamoya Kimeu (ca. 1940–   ) went to work in the 1950s as a common laborer with Louis and Mary Leakey's expeditions, having been talked into it by his uncle. At first he had little idea of the purpose of the extensive diggings or exactly what the Leakeys intended to do with "bones like stone" (fossils). Indeed, at first he thought they were digging up bones of recently deceased people, something strongly forbidden by his Kamba culture.

When Louis began to explain to Kamoya and the other workers what they were supposed to do (and equally important with delicate fossils, what *not* to do), he spoke in Kikuyu. (Fortunately, the Kamba language was similar.) As he tried to understand the instructions, Kimeu also responded to the fact that Louis did not sound like most white men— indeed, it was almost like listening to a tribal elder.

The laborers did not feel the same way about Mary. While they respected her, she came across in a more imperious and businesslike way. She also became very angry if someone made a mistake, especially if they accidentally knocked a chip off a fossil!

Unlike most of the other workers, Kimeu came to enjoy fossil hunting for its own sake—and he was very good at it. In 1963, he joined Richard Leakey, becoming an invaluable part of the exploration of the Omo River and Lake Rudolf (now Lake Turkana) sites. Among his finds were two spectacular specimens, a *Homo habilis* skull (designated KNM ER 813) and a famous *Homo erectus* known as Turkana Boy. Two fossil primates now bear his name.

In 1977, Kimeu became the curator in charge of prehistoric sites for the National Museum of Kenya.

MORE FINDS

Each day, Mary and Louis would confer by radio, but it was clear that it was Mary who was in charge of operations. On school holidays, Mary would be joined by her teenage sons, Richard and Jonathan.

One day, Jonathan discovered the jawbone of an animal they had not encountered before at Olduvai—probably a saber-toothed cat. (This was not his first discovery. Three years earlier, Jonathan had found the jawbone of a giant extinct baboon.)

An artist's impression of a *Homo habilis* camp *(London Art Archive/Alamy)*

By radio, Louis praised his son and suggested he dig some more—perhaps the rest of the cat's skeleton might be found. Instead, he found something better: a hominin tooth and toe bone. Now joined by Mary, son and mother began to excavate at what was now called Jonny's site.

All together they found 14 foot bones—probably the oldest early hominin foot and certainly the most complete one. They also found some finger bones, a collarbone, and a few tantalizing bits of skull. Later, they found some parietals (bones from the top of the skull). When Jonathan showed them to his mother, she instantly saw that the skull did not have a sagittal crest like "Zinj." When Jonathan unearthed a lower jaw filled with teeth, there was no mistaking that this was another type of hominin entirely. (Later, it would be assigned to the species *Homo habilis*.)

TREE OR BUSH?

The discovery of two clearly different hominin species in the same location (and thus time frame) confirmed what Louis had been arguing for years. Most researchers of the day still believed that at any given time and place there could be only one hominin species, because whatever new advantages it had evolved would allow it to eliminate potential competitors. Thus, human evolution was thought to go in a straight line, like the familiar cartoon showing the human species walking single file with a shambling near-ape at the back of the line and gradually progressing to a spear-carrying near man, a Neanderthal with club in hand, and then a modern human carrying, perhaps, a briefcase.

What Jonathan and Mary found suggested that the human family tree, rather than simply having ape and human branches in orderly sequence, was more like a bush with many shoots. Thus, rather than, for example, there being one type of *Australopithecus* at a time, followed by the first humans, it is now believed that several types of australopithecines and an early human such as *Homo habilis* shared the world for hundreds of thousands of years.

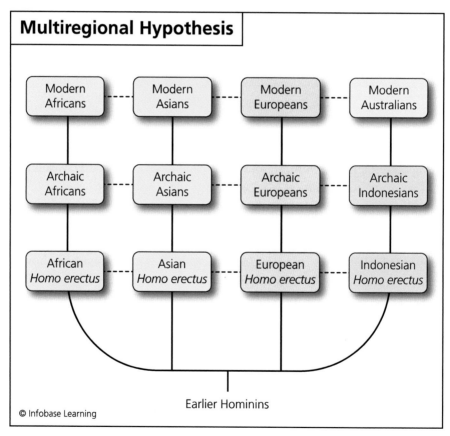

Multiregional Hypothesis

| Modern Africans | Modern Asians | Modern Europeans | Modern Australians |

| Archaic Africans | Archaic Asians | Archaic Europeans | Archaic Indonesians |

| African *Homo erectus* | Asian *Homo erectus* | European *Homo erectus* | Indonesian *Homo erectus* |

Earlier Hominins

© Infobase Learning

The *multiregional hypothesis* suggests that after the earliest human ancestors migrated from Africa they developed independently into different populations of modern humans.

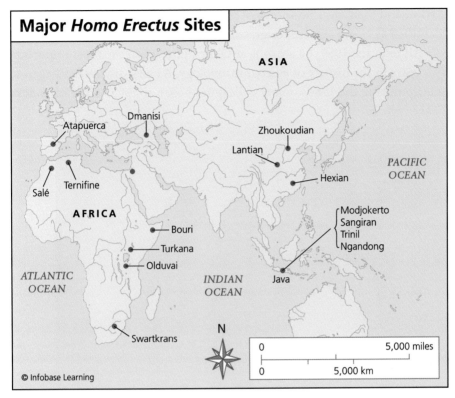

Major *Homo Erectus* Sites

Homo erectus was evidently a versatile species, migrating throughout Africa, Europe, and Asia, as far as Java.

One more surprise awaited them. One day in December 1960, Louis was looking back at the site where they had found "Zinj." He had a premonition or hunch that a skull was going to turn up. When he saw the rounded tops of bones sticking out of the soil, he reminded himself that it might just be a tortoise shell (which, when partly buried, can look a lot like a skull). However, his hunch was right: It was a hominin skull and quite different from "Zinj."

Louis called it the Chellean skull, referring to the hypothetical *culture* behind the stone hand axes he had been studying for so many years. Although he did not know it at the time, what he had found was the first African specimen of *Homo erectus,* an early *Homo* who had been found in Java and China in the 19th and early 20th centuries. Now, the Leakeys had found it in Africa. Louis had always maintained that Africa was the cradle of humanity, and today most researchers accept the theory that *H. erectus* did originate in

Africa, and then, over hundreds of thousands of years, it, or a later species identified as *Homo ergaster,* migrated deep into Asia and Europe.

All told, the 1959–60 seasons at Olduvai had been the most important two years in the history of paleoanthropology. As new discoveries began to pile up during the 1960s, many colleagues began to refer to the legendary Leakey's luck.

A Time of Transition

The mid-1960s and early 1970s would be a time of challenge and change for the Leakey family.

As he grew older, Louis began to suffer from declining health. But while he might have looked like an old lion—white-haired, overweight, arthritic, and down to a few teeth—the lion who was Louis Leakey could still roar out anthropological challenges while defending what he considered to be his turf.

The fossil that Jonathan had found back in 1960 was now being called *Homo habilis,* a name meaning "handyman," a fit name for the early tool-maker. Acceptance of this nomenclature would grow (in large part thanks to finds by Richard Leakey and his team), though just which specimens belong to the species remains a source of contention.

RICHARD STARTS OUT

A different source of conflict for Louis would be closer to home—his son Richard. His brothers had pretty much left the scene. Philip went to school in England, but soon abandoned his education and eventually bounced around among a number of jobs. Jonathan, who had shown such promise as a fossil-finder, became a herpetologist (snake specialist).

As for Richard, his father told him that he could either pursue his education with parental blessing or support himself. Perhaps appropriately for the son of a man who had moved into his own hut as a teenager, Richard decided to strike out on his own.

Taking advantage of the experience gained from growing up with a familiarity with the animals and landscape of Africa, Richard first developed a business trapping and selling wild animals. Later, he supplemented this by meeting the demand from scientists and museums for animal specimens. He collected animal carcasses, boiled them down until only bones remained, then bleached and carefully labeled the bones for sale. A third business arose when Richard spent a season managing the Leakey camp at

JANE GOODALL, PIONEER PRIMATOLOGIST

Jane Morris Goodall (1934–   ) has studied chimpanzees for more than half a century. Her first chimpanzee was a realistic-looking stuffed toy. While some adults thought the toy would frighten her, it had the opposite effect, kindling a love for animals—and chimps in particular.

Pursuing her fascination with animals (especially in Africa), Goodall visited a farm in the Kenyan highlands in 1957. She decided to stay in Kenya, getting a job as a secretary. One day, she rather boldly telephoned Louis Leakey, asking for an appointment to talk with him about animals.

Unknown to her, Louis had, for a long time, been trying to get a primate study project going. He believed that important clues to understanding the way prehistoric primates and human ancestors might have behaved would be found by studying the behavior of living primates.

Louis offered Goodall the opportunity to work as his own secretary and took her to Olduvai to show her his work. The next year, he paid to send her to London to gain some formal training in primate behavior and anatomy. In 1960, having raised more funds, he arranged for her (and her mother Vanne) to go to the Gombe Stream National Park in Tanganyika (now Tanzania) to begin to work with chimpanzees. Louis also arranged for a period of advanced education at Cambridge, resulting in her earning a doctorate in ethology (animal behavior) despite her lack of a prior degree. Her dissertation was on the behavior of the free-range chimpanzee, based on her experience at Gombe.

Jane was the first of the group of prominent woman primatologists sometimes known as Leakey's Angels. Although Louis expressed a romantic interest in her for a time, she apparently was able to decline without affecting his extensive support for her work.

Olduvai and then turned the experience into becoming a safari guide with his own company.

MARITAL WOES

Another reason why Richard and his brothers may have needed some distance from their parents was that the Leakey marriage was far from happy

Goodall's subsequent studies have looked at virtually every aspect of primate behavior. She has said that she believes chimps are over all "rather nicer" than humans, but she has also discussed the dark side of their behavior, including vicious warfare.

In 1977, she founded the Jane Goodall Institute for the study and protection of chimpanzees. The foundation is now an international education and advocacy group. She is a fierce advocate for animal welfare and rights and has attacked the conditions under which primates are kept in zoos.

Goodall has received many honors including being appointed as a Dame Commander of the Order of the British Empire in 2002.

Jane Goodall was the first of three women (later dubbed "Leakey's Angels") whose scientific careers owe much to Louis Leakey's interest (professional or otherwise). She is best known as an expert on and advocate for chimpanzees. Here, though, she is studying an African baboon. *(Photo by Fotos International/ Getty Images)*

Birute Mary Galdikas, the third of Leakey's Angels, and an assistant prepare to release an orangutan named Isabel into the wild at Tanjung Puting National Park on Borneo Island, Indonesia. (*AP Images*)

during the time they were growing up. Louis was genuinely inspirational and helpful to young people he saw as being talented and whom he thought could carry out needed research. The complication was that most of these protégées were women, and Louis often fell in love with them—and other women besides.

The three most famous women in this group, who became known as Leakey's Angels, were Jane Goodall, Dian Fossey, and Birute Galdikas. Leakey had a certain mission behind his encouraging the three: All would study primates (chimpanzees, gorillas, and orangutans respectively). Louis believed that understanding the behavior of modern primates would go a long way to figuring out how earlier primates and human ancestors might have lived. All three women achieved success. Goodall became the world's best-known authority on chimps and, in recent years, has become a staunch advocate for conservation and animal rights. Fossey, known for her work with the gentle giants (mountain gorillas) met a tragic death, probably at the hands of the poachers from whom she tried to protect her primate subjects. Finally, Galdikas has achieved a similar degree of expertise and protectiveness with regard to the orangutan.

DIAN FOSSEY, FRIEND OF THE MOUNTAIN GORILLAS

Zoologist and primatologist Dian Fossey (1932–85) was born and grew up in San Francisco, California. Her interest in veterinary medicine was thwarted by difficulty with courses in chemistry and physics, so she changed her specialty to occupational therapy and began to build a career in that field.

Fossey had always been quite interested in Africa, and in 1963 she put together enough money to pay for a seven-week tour of the continent. Her tour included Olduvai Gorge, where she met Louis and Mary Leakey. Louis told her about the importance of primate research—Jane Goodall had already established a successful program studying chimpanzees. At her next stop (in Uganda), Fossey encountered mountain gorillas for the first time and was quite taken with them.

Encouraged by Leakey (with whom she apparently had a brief affair), Fossey began an intensive study of the gorillas in their natural habitat at Virunga National Park in Rwanda. By 1980, she had written extensively

(continues)

Dian Fossey, another of Leakey's Angels, who fought to save endangered mountain gorillas like these in Rwanda's Virunga Mountains from poachers *(AP Images)*

> *(continued)*
>
> about the animals' family life, often finding them to be gentle, unlike the King Kong stereotype. As she became particularly attached to individual gorillas, her opposition to the poachers who threatened the species' survival grew. She organized antipoaching patrols to destroy traps and tried to prevent the export of the animals to zoos. When her favorite gorilla, named Digit, was killed by a poacher in 1979, Fossey created the Digit Fund International to raise funds for antipoaching efforts.
>
> On December 26, 1985, Dian was found murdered in her cabin in Virunga. The last entry in her diary read, "When you realize the value of all life, you dwell less on what is past and concentrate on the future." Her killer or killers were never identified.

Of the three, only Fossey apparently had a romantic relationship with Louis. (Louis did not let personal rejection stop him from continuing to support the others' education and work.) Mary, of course, was upset at the depth of these relationships, but she was more upset by Louis's more casual affairs. In *Disclosing the Past,* Mary described how she would come home to their house only to find that Louis had female company. In turn, Mary often consoled herself with drink, and the result could be a shouting match or days of cold silence.

CALICO MIRAGE?

Another source of Mary's growing disenchantment with Louis was the latter's involvement with a controversial site on the other side of the world. Louis normally had little time for or interest in human fossils outside of Africa. The one exception began in 1959 when he met an American archaeologist named Ruth DeEtte Simpson (1918–2000). She showed him some artifacts that looked like stone scrapers. They had been found at a site called Calico Hills, outside of Barstow, California.

The geological layer in which the supposed tools were found was dated to as much as 200,000 years ago. If they were real tools, they would push the time of the first human settlements in the New World back about 10 times from the commonly accepted date of around 20,000 years before the present.

In October 1970, Louis organized an international conference to discuss the tools. The whole affair proved rather embarrassing. Many of Louis's friends and colleagues, as well as Mary, wanted nothing to do with it. Indeed, Mary thought that Louis's involvement in Calico showed his mental deterioration.

The current view of experts is that the tools are not artifacts but geofacts, produced by ancient streams pressuring the rocks and flaking pieces off them, as well as the effects of erosion, weather, and other natural factors. The clincher would seem to be the complete failure to find any human fossils in the area.

RICHARD TURNS TOWARD PALEOANTHROPOLOGY

By the mid-1960s, Richard had decided to become involved again with fossil hunting. In 1966, he married Margaret Cropper, who he had met in Olduvai in 1961. When Margaret went to Scotland to get an advanced degree, Richard, who had not even graduated from high school, followed her, trying to catch up with basic education. However, Richard soon decided that there was little in school that he really needed. Richard and Margaret began to quarrel: Margaret was evidently upset that Richard was not serious about education and wanted to use the family reputation as a key to the career door. In 1969, the couple divorced.

Meanwhile Meave Epps had attracted Richard's attention. She was a specialist in monkeys, working in the Tigoni Primate Research Center that had been set up by Louis. Richard, who, for a time, was also interested in monkey fossils, hired Meave to write a paper about a specimen.

During summer 1967, Richard worked with an international expedition in the Omo Valley in Ethiopia where he found two rather battered skulls that later turned out to belong to early *H. sapiens*. On a return flight to Nairobi, Richard made a discovery that would be of greater importance to his future. When a thunderstorm came up and the pilot flew around it, they found themselves over the eastern shore of Lake Rudolf (now Lake Turkana). Richard saw some sediments that looked like the kind likely to have many fossils. The next day, he hired a helicopter pilot to take him down to the sediments and quickly found some fossils. Although he discovered he had neglected to pinpoint the location he had surveyed, in spring 1968 he fired off a proposal for further exploration of the area to the National Geographic Society. He was granted funding, but since the competing proposal was from his father

Lake Turkana in northern Kenya *(Richard Human/Alamy)*

the result was not good for that particular relationship. Richard also used his family connections to secure a position at the National Museum of Kenya, despite his lack of academic credentials.

EXPEDITION TO KOOBI FORA

Later that year, Richard, now aided by Meave and a geology graduate student named Kay Behrensmeyer, began to hunt fossils in earnest. Their site, Koobi Fora, was a little peninsula that jutted out into Lake Turkana, the largest permanent desert lake in the world.

Today, Koobi Fora is a fiercely hot, stark, and bleak desert once away from the lakeshore. However, for the human ancestors of almost 2 million years ago, the area must have been incredibly prolific with animal life. A river flowed through it, in which crocodiles and giant turtles swam and huge hippos splashed. The surrounding area was grassland, then forest, inhabited by giant pigs, rhinos, giraffes (with necks much shorter than today), and predators such as the saber-tooth tiger.

Much to the delight of future paleontologists, a nearby volcano periodically erupted, belching ash and lava into the surrounding area. The result is a series of ash layers that can be used to date the fossils that formed near them. (In his autobiography *One Life*, Richard noted that as a result of all this geological help, "One of our biggest problems was the sheer quantity of fossils!")

Desert soil is very fragile, and the Land Rovers that had become ubiquitous for explorers could easily crush fossils on or just beneath the surface. For a while, Richard toyed with an imaginative idea: Why not use camels instead? However, they found after a short trial that this idea only traded one problem for several others. Camels are famously uncooperative beasts. Further, both packs of hungry lions and gangs of thieves were attracted to a camel caravan. One time, a large gang armed with rifles confronted Richard, who was on his way to gather water. Trying to appear nonchalant, Richard raised his own rifle over his head, filled his water container, and went back to camp. The camels were soon out of a job.

Besides completing surveys that suggested a bright future for fossil hunting at Koobi Fora, Richard made one significant find on this trip—the *cranium* of *Australopithecus boisei* (the name then also used for Mary's original "Dear Boy"). Mary, who was visiting the camp, praised her son lavishly.

LOUIS'S LAST YEARS

In 1970, Richard consolidated his position at the National Museum, becoming its director. He immediately began a five-year plan for expanding the facilities, establishing education and wildlife conservation programs. The budget for prehistoric research, on which Louis among others depended, also came under Richard's control.

Until then, all significant posts at the museum were held by foreigners. Richard believed that it was time for Kenyan citizens (of which he was one, of course) to be in charge.

Despite their growing animosity, Louis and Richard did have something in common—serious health problems. In January 1970, Louis, in Olduvai, had a heart attack and tried to shrug it off as he had so many other health issues. He flew to London, where he always stayed with Vanne Goodall (Jane's mother). Vanne, concerned about what had happened, insisted on calling a doctor. After being put in a hospital, Louis had a second, more severe heart attack. It would be six months before Louis could return to Kenya.

The following January, Louis had another sort of attack. While visiting some historic ruins, something evidently disturbed a huge nest of bees, which swarmed all over Louis. Besides falling and hitting his head and injuring his leg, Louis received about 800 bee stings. For a while he seemed near death, but he eventually recovered.

While Louis seemed to recover physically, his mental health took a turn for the worse. Louis was already upset over how Richard had taken over the museum, especially the funding for prehistoric research and the Centre for Prehistory and Paleontology that Louis had founded. Richard's plans for the expansion of the museum sometimes ran roughshod over Louis's friends who were involved with the institution. Later, in *One Life* Richard would admit that

> I was doing the right thing but largely for the wrong reasons; in other words, I was acting at least partly out of spite [against Louis] even though the program I initiated did benefit the Museum and Kenya.

In *Ancestral Passions,* Virginia Morell writes that

> The ongoing quarrels between father and son were now legendary, and for every fossil discovery that drew them together, some new administrative issue cast them farther apart.

Despite having considerable justification for his feelings, Louis's response to Richard's activity began to veer into paranoia. In general, his mind seemed to be failing even as his body declined.

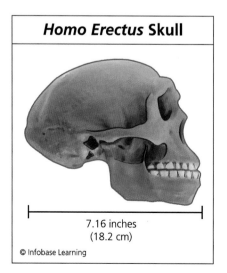

Homo Erectus Skull

7.16 inches
(18.2 cm)

© Infobase Learning

A drawing that shows the shape and scale of a *Homo erectus* skull. This early human species had a considerably larger brain size than a chimpanzee, but still small compared to modern humans.

Richard Leakey with three hominin (ancestral human) skulls *(Danita Delimont/Alamy)*

Louis would receive a respite from his health problems. After he fell and hit his head during a conference in 1971, surgeons found and removed two blood clots from his brain. The results were remarkable: Louis could now walk and move much more easily, and he also seemed much clearer mentally. This improvement allowed the Leakeys to share a wonderful moment. Richard brought to Mary and Louis one of his major finds, Skull KNM-ER 1470, a *H. erectus* or *H. rudolfensis* initially dated at the time to 2.6 million years ago. Louis in particular was delighted with Richard's find. For decades, he had searched for proof of his belief that the evolutionary line leading to *modern humans* went back much farther than his rivals would admit. Skull 1470 seemed to be just the kind of convincing proof needed.

Louis soon left Nairobi for London, where Vanne Goodall helped him finish his autobiography *By the Evidence,* covering the period following that in the earlier *White African.* When he began to feel unusually exhausted, Louis went to a doctor who performed tests. The doctor found no heart problems but urged Louis not to go back to Kenya for a few days. On October 1, 1972, Louis collapsed and died.

Unknown to nearly everyone, Richard had been suffering from a serious health crisis of his own. Back in 1968, when he went to the doctor complaining of a persistent sore throat, Richard with diagnosed with a kidney disease resulting from the throat infection. The doctor said Richard needed six weeks of bed rest, but having just established himself at the National Museum of Kenya, Richard decided this was no time to leave his work.

The following spring, while visiting the United States, Richard saw a kidney specialist who told him that it was only a matter of time (months or years) before his kidneys would fail. That would leave him a choice of dialysis or transplant. Dialysis would essentially mean not being more than a couple days away from a machine that was not even available in most of Africa, let alone in the field. As for a transplant, he would need a donor with a matching organ who would be willing to undergo major surgery—and there would always be the risk that his body's immune system would reject the new kidney.

Changes for Richard and Mary

With Louis gone and Mary working relatively quietly in Olduvai, Richard was now becoming the lead Leakey in the ever-shifting arena of paleoanthropology.

Richard had found a way to get around his lack of academic credentials. As important finds such as Skull 1470 came to light, Richard made sure the popular press (notably *National Geographic,* which was also a major funding source) had the latest information. Richard also arranged for the scientists on his team to write scholarly papers about the find. Even though he had no degree, Richard would be listed as coauthor. As researchers became used to the fact that Richard was indeed knowledgeable (even if not a specialist), as well as being an experienced and successful fossil hunter, his lack of a Ph.D became much less important.

HOW OLD IS SKULL 1470?

Aided largely by Meave's skill in piecing together the fragments, Skull 1470 was prepared for its scientific debut at a conference held by the Zoological Society of London. A rather sour note was struck, as recalled by Richard in *One Life,* when Lord Zuckerman, hosting the event, congratulated his find but referred to him as "an amateur and not a specialist." He thanked both Richard and his father for their achievements "not as geochemists or anything else, but just as people interested in collecting fossils on which specialists can work."

By the 1980s at Lake Turkana, Richard Leakey had truly come into his own as a paleontologist and organizer of expeditions. Here, he is holding the skull 1470 (an *Australopithecus*) in his right hand and the skull of a *Homo habilis* in his left hand. *(Marion Kaplan/Alamy)*

Whatever subtle snub these remarks might have represented, the popular media attending the conference had a quite different view. A mob of reporters and photographers surrounded Richard to ask him about Skull 1470.

The slighted professionals would perhaps get their revenge. Again, as with Louis at Kanam and Kanjera, the problem was dating. Early in the Koobi Fora digging, Richard had arranged for two expert British geochronologists, Frank Fitch and Jack Miller, to date the volcanic rock or *tuff* from the site where Skull 1470 and some stone tools had been found.

Back when Louis began his career, layers such as volcanic deposits could only be used to identify the relative age of fossils. Clearly, in a geologically undisturbed site, lower layers or beds of sediment were laid down longer ago than ones nearer the surface. Combined with other data (such as tools from a known cultural period or animals that had become extinct after a given time), an approximate date could be assigned to a fossil.

By the 1970s, however, dating by means of radioactive decay was being used. When volcanic ash such as that at Koobi Fora is first produced, it contains potassium, a certain portion of which is in radioactive form. Over time, the radioactive potassium steadily decays into another radioactive element or

DONALD JOHANSON, DISCOVERER OF LUCY

Donald Carl Johanson, (1943–   ), an American paleoanthropologist, ranks alongside the Leakeys in the pursuit of knowledge of human origins. Born in Chicago, Johanson earned his advanced degrees in anthropology at the University of Chicago. At the time of his discovery of Lucy (in 1974), Johanson was on the faculty at Case Western Reserve University.

The discovery of Lucy in Hadar, Ethiopia, was, like so much in paleoanthropology, a matter of good luck. He and a graduate student, Tom Gray, had grown tired of paperwork in camp and had decided to survey the area a bit.

Lucy, a small, graceful australopithecine, quickly captured the popular imagination. (Johanson's team later found several other similar hominins, which became known as the First Family.) As Johanson became a celebrity, he and Mary and Richard Leakey began to publicly quarrel. In 1981, Johanson established the Institute of Human Origins in Berkeley, California.

Johanson believes his research places Lucy (A. *afarensis*) directly in the line of evolution leading to humanity. (As with many other issues in paleoanthropology, there are competing theories.)

Johanson has written several books beginning with *Lucy: The Beginnings of Humankind* (coauthored with Maitland Edey).

A rising star (and Leakey rival) in paleontology, Donald Johanson is shown with a recreation of Lucy (*Australopithecus afarensis*) at the "Lucy's Legacy: The Hidden Treasures of Ethiopia" exhibit at the Discovery Times Square Exposition in New York City, June 24, 2009. (*AP Images*)

form of argon. By measuring the ratio of argon to potassium, it is possible to estimate when the ash was originally formed—which also means the approximate time any fossil or tool associated with it must have been deposited.

Miller and Fitch offered to use a newer, more sensitive version of potassium-argon dating on the Koobi Fora samples. They told Richard that the method, while considerably more expensive, would give a more accurate, definitive date. When the results came back, they dated the tuff at 2.6 million years old, plus or minus 0.26 million (that is, 260,000 years). A later test came back with a date a bit more recent—2.42 million years.

This date was just fine with Richard: It would make Skull 1470 almost 2.5 million years old, pushing the line of humanlike ancestors back, just as Louis had always claimed it should be.

However, another method, matching the tuff to pig fossils (a method that had also caused Louis trouble), gave a more recent date—2 million years old or less. Further, potassium-argon tests from other labs eventually came up with later dates. The controversy over the age of KBS (the name of the site where Skull 1470 was found) became part of nearly every conference during the 1970s.

In 1976, Tim White (1950–   ), a paleoanthropologist who had worked both with Richard at Koobi Fora and with Donald Johanson (of Lucy fame), coauthored a report that dated KBS to less than 2 million years. Richard was upset—not, he insisted, because of the late date, but because the report referred to some fossils that had not been published by their finders—generally considered a breach of scientific etiquette. Although the report was rewritten to remove the material to which Richard objected, White continued to complain to colleagues about Richard's heavy-handed censorship.

Finally, in 1980, Richard admitted that he was wrong about the date of KBS and thus of Skull 1470. He said that while he regretted the damage to formerly friendly relationships with some close colleagues, the controversy had at least resulted in improving the dating techniques.

MORE FROM KOOBI FORA

Richard and Meave, now with two daughters, continued the work at Koobi Fora, as well as establishing an institution called the Foundation for Research into the Origin of Man (FROM), making television documentaries. and writing two books with coauthor Roger Lewin.

At Koobi Fora, Richard depended on the skills of Kamoya Kimeu, a Kenyan who had become a master fossil-hunter. In August 1975, another keen eye, that of Bernard Ngeneo, spied a hominin brow ridge. Richard carefully began to excavate as documentary filmmakers recorded their progress. A skull now known as KNM-ER-3733 was revealed. It is now attributed to either *H. erectus* or *H. ergaster,* depending on which scientist one asks. The specimen, believed to be a young adult female, would add much to the study of the early humans who would so successfully populate three continents.

IN THE FOOTSTEPS OF ANCESTORS

After Louis's passing, Mary, always the quieter of the two, was content to continue her work without fanfare. Way back in 1935, an African stranger had approached her and Louis. He said that he knew of a place with "bones

Mary Leakey at the Laetoli, Tanzania, excavation site in 1978: It was here that famous Laetoli footprints were unearthed. *(John Reader/Photo Researchers, Inc.)*

like stone," later returning with some actual fossils. Mary and Louis took what was then a two-day trip south from Olduvai to Laetoli. They indeed found some fossils, but while Laetoli went on their list of future projects, they had never seemed to find time for it.

Now, 40 years later, Mary had moved her operation down to Laetoli from Olduvai, despite the difficulties in working at such a remote place. At the time, Mary did not realize the significance of an unusual geological feature at Laetoli.

About 3.6 million years ago, a nearby volcano called Sadiman erupted and threw up enough ash to blanket Laetoli. It then rained, and the ash, which had just the right mineral composition and consistency, turned into something rather like wet cement. This made it perfect for capturing the footprints of any creature walking in the area. Even more fortunately, the volcano then produced more ash layers that covered the prints and preserved them indefinitely.

In September 1976, some of the Laetoli fossil hunters were taking a break from working in the hot sun. One of them, a biologist named David Western, started one of his favorite games—an elephant dung fight. (The dry dung formed something with the heft of a large, puffy snowball.) As the fight spread, others, including Philip Leakey and Kay Behrensmeyer, joined in. When two of them, Kay and paleoanthropologist Andrew Hill, ducked into a little gully to take cover from an attack, they noticed footprints of elephants and an antelope perfectly preserved in the ancient, hardened ash.

More of these prints soon turned up or were uncovered. Spreading before their eyes was a picture of exactly what animals had crossed the area over a day or two . . . nearly 4 million years ago! It also gradually dawned on them that any hominins traveling in the area would also have left their prints behind. With Mary urging caution and careful investigation, they indeed began to find and follow a trail of footprints of human ancestors.

In fact, there appeared to be two sets of prints leading along the ancient trail. One set seemed large (indeed, feet larger than could easily be attributed to a known hominin species). The large prints had a peculiar impression in the heel, as though perhaps their maker had damaged his or her foot and was limping or dragging it. The other set of prints were much smaller.

At first they thought that there were just these two hominins, but a visitor, wildlife photographer Alan Root, came up with a different explanation. The peculiar double marks in the larger prints could be explained by a third person stepping carefully in the larger prints—a way of walking practiced by some native peoples today. Thus, the rather romantic picture was painted of the scene: The group might have been a family—father, mother, and child?

The famous trail of hominin footprints preserved in volcanic ash at Laetoli. The prints belong to two adults, with possibly a child walking in the footsteps of one of the adults. The prints to the far right belong to a hipparion, an extinct three-toed horse. *(John Reader/Photo Researchers, Inc.)*

Mary asked for some help in working further on the prints. She enlisted the aid of Donald Johanson, who was at this time still on friendly terms with the Leakeys, as well as Tim White, whose differences (with Mary, at least) had been patched up.

CONTENTION IN SWEDEN

The big star at the 1978 Nobel Symposium at the Royal Swedish Academy of Sciences would be Donald Johanson. In 1973, Johanson had discovered Lucy in the Afar region of Ethiopia. This fossil, which Johanson and Tim White had given the name *Australopithecus afarensis,* is probably the most famous fossil find of all. (The name Lucy arose because Johanson's team had been listening to a recording of the Beatles' song "Lucy in the Sky with Diamonds.")

The news of Lucy and a subsequent group of fossils dubbed the First Family was the prehistoric sensation of the decade. Besides anything Richard might have felt about being pushed out of the limelight, there was a fundamental conflict between what Johanson presented to the meeting and what the Leakeys had always stood for.

Mary, like Louis, had always considered australopithecines to be off the evolutionary trail leading to humans. Now Johanson and White, seeing similarities between Lucy and her kin and fossils Mary had found at Laetoli, had implicitly put them all in the *Australopithecus* genus. Mary was indignant about this: As quoted in *Ancestral Passions,* she snapped at Johanson and White, saying, "Call it what you like, call it *Hylobates,* call it *Symphalangus,* call it anything, but don't call it *Australopithecus.*"

Now they were doing just that. What was equally offensive to Mary was that they had used a fossil from the Laetoli collection as the *holotype* for their new species—the reference fossil that would be used for future comparisons. Although the normal practice was to use the first fossil found of a species as the holotype, and Mary's find was earlier, she thought that her Laetoli fossils would be swallowed up into *A. afarensis* together with Lucy and the First Family.

Finally, there was what Mary considered to be the final insult from Johanson. In his presentation, he talked rather extensively about Mary's find of hominin footprints at Laetoli. Mary had thought that she would get to introduce the find (it was her team's, after all). After Johanson spoke, Mary found herself with most of what she had intended to say already having been said. The embarrassment of having to find something else to say only added to her discomfort and anger. The incident would be a major part of the break between the Leakeys and the Johanson/White partnership. (Richard would have his own confrontation with them later.)

CRISIS FOR RICHARD

As the 1970s drew to an end, Richard's kidney problems had grown much worse. People could not help but notice that he looked bloated and had great trouble walking any distance or climbing stairs. Finally, he had to choose, and he chose the transplant option.

Despite the considerable acrimony that had developed between Richard and his brothers Jonathan and Philip, both brothers offered him a kidney, as did his half-brother, Colin (son of Louis and Frida), as well as some friends.

Philip proved to be the best match. He had seldom been in Richard's life, having lived among various African tribes and tried many different jobs and schemes for making money. Philip agreed to donate a kidney, but he was running for election to the Kenyan parliament and wanted to wait until after the election.

Richard agreed to wait, but the election kept getting delayed and his health steadily worsened. Richard kept up a good face, insisting he could manage, but Meave knew how sick he really was. As a Kenyan in Britain, he had to wait for access to dialysis—when he was finally hooked up to the machine the result was a great improvement in his health.

On November 29, 1979, the operation was finally performed. (As they were rolled on gurneys into the operating room, Richard had offered Philip a final chance to back out.) The operation itself was a success, with Richard noting that he could no longer hate Philip's guts because he now had part of them!

The operation was successful, yes, but the powerful drugs given to suppress rejection also suppress the immune system, making the patient very vulnerable to infection. About a month after the surgery, Richard was back in the hospital with pneumonia and septicemia. For a day he lay near death—later he reported he had had an out of body experience in which only Meave's calm presence had urged him to cling to life.

LEAKEY V. JOHANSON, ROUND TWO

In February 1980, Richard was finally able to return to Kenya, where he soon returned to a whirlwind of projects. He struggled to keep the museum afloat in the complex world of postcolonial Kenyan politics while planning a new expedition to Lake Turkana.

Meanwhile, Donald Johanson had published *Lucy: The Beginnings of Humankind,* written with Maitland Edey. While his writing praised the Leakeys to some extent, both Richard and Mary felt many of the stories Johanson had told about them were inaccurate and unfair. The days of collaboration and friendship between the eminent paleoanthropologists were clearly over.

The media continued to portray the rivalry as a clash between the reigning first family of archaeology and the bright young upstart. (Americans in particular tended to identify with Johanson as one of their own.) In spring 1981, it was arranged for Richard to appear on a television program hosted by famed broadcaster Walter Cronkite. He had been told that the topic was to be the conflict between evolution and creationism. However, when he arrived (and it was too late to back out gracefully), he found that what was really intended was a debate between him and Johanson over human origins.

Cronkite began by introducing Johanson as the man who had found Lucy and thus had passed the Leakeys in the race to find the so-called missing link between ape and human. Johanson was equipped with casts of his fossils and a chart illustrating his belief that the human line had evolved from *A. afarensis.* Richard had no such props to present his side—he had come directly from a meeting and had no reason to think such things would be needed.

As Johanson presented his material, Richard became increasingly uncomfortable. Finally, when Johanson showed his version of the human family tree and the time came for Richard to explain his version, he simply crossed out Johanson's chart with a marker and put in a question mark, saying that there was not enough in the fossil record to draw any such conclusion. The split between the two men had become permanent.

TURKANA BOY AND THE BLACK SKULL

During all this time, Richard's well-organized team of fossil hunters, known as the Hominid Gang, had continued working. In summer 1984, Kamoya Kimeu, the team's leader (and Richard's close friend), called. He had found a piece of hominin skull on the slope of narrow gully. The next day, they began to sift through the material at the site, but nothing seemed to be turning up. Richard and some of the others had wandered off when shouts called them back. "Lots of skull" had been found.

The bone pieces were sent back to Meave for analysis, and the digging continued. Their work was hampered by the extensive roots of a wait-a-bit

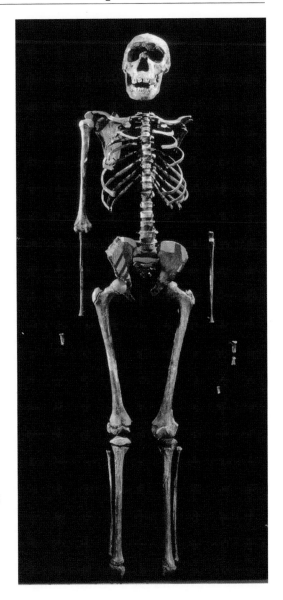

The skeleton of Turkana Boy, a young *Homo ergaster* (or possibly *Homo erectus*) discovered in 1984 by Komaya Kimeu, part of a team led by Richard Leakey *(Danita Delimont/ Alamy)*

thornbush that kept poking at Richard. Soon, Richard and his assistant Peter Nzube suddenly saw half of an upper jaw entangled in the roots.

Meanwhile Meave and another researcher, Alan Walker, had determined that the bones had actually come from a child. The key bit of evidence was a missing third molar—missing because it had not yet grown in. (They checked their theory by peering into the mouth of Richard and Meave's daughter Louise, 12 years old at the time!)

For the next few weeks, they experienced what Richard in *Origins Reconsidered* described as "paleontological bliss." They soon accumulated an astonishingly complete skeleton of *H. ergaster*. The picture that emerged was of a remarkably tall (five feet, three inches [1.6 m]) boy. (It is now estimated that he was about eight years old, but due to more rapid development than in modern humans, he was probably the equivalent of a teenager.) While his species had a brain capacity somewhat smaller than the norm for modern humans, they made stone tools and perhaps had a rudimentary language. Remarkably, an analysis of a section of bone from the skeleton suggested that the individual, soon called Turkana Boy, had died from an excess of vitamin A, probably from excessive consumption of a prize prehistoric delicacy—raw liver!

About a year after Turkana Boy, in August 1985, Alan Walker dug around a piece of skull Kamoya Kimeu had found a few days earlier. The piece became a partial skull that was called the Black Skull because of the color it had acquired from manganese salts in the surrounding soil. The assembled skull was a real puzzle, though the large tooth roots suggested something in *Australopithecus*. (Today, the consensus favors *Paranthropus aethiopicus*, the *Paranthropus* designation having displaced *Australopithecus* in many cases, though Tim White still favors the latter for this specimen.)

MARY RETIRES

By the beginning of the 1980s, Mary's long career had brought her many honors. In 1981, she received an honorary degree from Oxford, a long ceremony she noted in *Disclosing the Past* was accompanied by much Latin, spoken "as if they understand it."

A few years later, Mary began to have health problems that made it difficult for her to work in the field, and anyway, political changes had closed the border between Kenya and Tanzania (where the Laetoli site was).

A blood clot behind her left eye left Mary partly blinded. Gradually, she learned to live with the disability, living with Richard and Meave until she could move into her own home in Langata.

Mary spent her remaining years mainly writing, with some travel. She died on December 9, 1996, at the age of 83.

RICHARD'S NEW CAREER

Following his triumphant finds at Turkana, Richard had to devote most of his time to museum affairs and increasingly Kenyan politics and a new goal—saving the endangered elephants. In 1989, Kenyan president Daniel Arap Moi asked Richard to reorganize the government's Department of Wildlife and Conservation.

The department was riddled with corruption and virtually bankrupt. Poaching, or the illegal taking of animals, was a roaring business. In particular, the well-armed gangs of poachers killed elephants, simply because of the value of their ivory tusks.

Although the task of forming a new Kenyan Wildlife Service was daunting, Richard threw himself into it as wholeheartedly as he had pursued fossils. Money had to be found to equip the new service with vehicles and planes for antipoaching patrols, as well as letting honest workers know that he would back them up.

Besides the moral obligation to protect one of the world's most intelligent and social animals, preventing the disappearance of the elephant was vital for tourism, a key industry in Kenya. Richard also had to decide what to do with a huge pile of confiscated elephant tusks. Selling the valuable ivory would have netted several million dollars for wildlife and other programs, but Richard decided to send a different message: he decided to burn the pile of tusks in a spectacular pyre.

There was one little problem. Ivory tusks are actually huge teeth, and as any fossil hunter knows, teeth are among the most durable parts of any animal. Ivory does not burn. Richard solved the problem by coating the tusks with a highly flammable liquid plastic, then piling them together with firewood and stuffing straw into the cracks. The resulting fire made worldwide news.

The tide seemed to be turning against the poachers, but the hazards of Kenyan politics remained. Richard kept receiving death threats, and he and his family had to have a permanent staff of bodyguards.

STRUGGLING ON

On June 2, 1993, Richard, an accomplished pilot, was flying four staff members to a meeting. Ten minutes into the flight, the engine cut out, and he suddenly was flying a heavy glider. Richard managed to guide the plane into an open field, but one wing clipped a tree, spinning them into the ground.

Richard's passengers were not seriously injured, but the story was different for him. Because of the possibility that the plane had been sabotaged, guards accompanied him to a Nairobi hospital room. Richard's left leg had to be amputated eight inches (20 cm) above the knee. Showing typical humor,

Richard and his daughter Anna joked about the whole thing—she suggested his next book (which became *Wildlife Wars*) be titled "one foot in the grave." Going along with the joke, Richard went on to ask for the amputated limb, saying that he would bury it at Koobi Fora, it being the only part of his funeral he would be able to attend.

The injuries were not really a laughing matter. Despite 14 operations, Richard's right leg did not seem to be able to be made functional, and he finally decided that it, too, would be amputated. Fitted with two artificial legs, Richard gradually learned to walk confidently, as well as drive.

As the century drew to an end, Richard continued his wildlife work and his involvement in Kenyan politics. He became involved with a reform movement that sought to unseat Moi's Kenya African National Union (KANU) party. In turn, he was accused of being a racist and traitor, and at one point Richard, struggling to get away on his artificial legs, was chased by a group of young men with whips. In 1999, Moi had to give in to the reformers and as part of a compromise appointed Richard to the position of cabinet secretary and head of the civil service. However that position did not last long.

Later, Richard left politics in favor of science and wildlife work. In 2002, he became a professor of anthropology at Stony Brook University in New York, heading the Turkana Basin Institute. Two years later, he founded (and still heads) an organization called Wildlife Direct. The purpose of the organization is to link worldwide supporters directly to African conservationists via blogs. When an insurgent uprising threatened the mountain gorillas in Virunga National Park in Congo in January 2007, Wildlife Direct was able to successfully organize the effort to protect them. That same year, Richard became the head of the Kenyan branch of Transparency International, an organization dedicated to exposing corporate influence and corruption in international development.

Conclusion: Legacies and Changes

Although there are likely to be disputes over fossil species for years to come, the legacy of the Leakeys to the scientific understanding of human origins can be summed up in what nearly everyone in the anthropological fields now agrees is true about humanity. Humans evolved their distinct characteristics from earlier primates over millions of years. Humans and their near relatives originated in Africa and only later spread out into the surrounding continents.

ENDURING EFFORT

Over decades of inspired exploration and difficult, sometimes dangerous, work, the Leakeys showed that hominin fossils could be found, pieced together, and studied in depth. Despite some improvements in transportation and communication, field researchers today essentially face the same difficulties and challenges that the Leakeys and their contemporaries did.

While Louis and Mary are gone and Richard has essentially moved on to other things, Louise (1972–   ), Richard and Meave's daughter, still works with fossils. When her father's plane crashed in 1993, Louise took over running the Turkana expedition and camp. Today, she works with her mother Meave at the Koobi Fora Research Project.

Not surprisingly, new hominin finds continue to be made in many parts of the world. Usually, the specimens are of a known species or at least look

Louise Leakey represents the latest generation of Leakeys to be making paleontological news. Here, she is shown with her mother, Meave Leakey, examining a *Homo erectus* skull from Lleret, Kenya in 2007. *(Ken Garrett/National Geographic/Getty Images)*

similar. But perhaps as a reminder that nothing should be taken for granted, one of the strangest hominins of all was discovered by archaeologist Mike Morwood and his team in 2004 on the island of Flores, Indonesia. Later, partial skeletons of a total of nine individuals were found.

The finders consider it to be a new species within the *Homo* genus, giving it the name *Homo floresiensis,* Because of their short stature of only about 3.5 feet (1.06 m) and small brain size, some critics have suggested that *H. floresiensis* were modern humans who had been victimized by some sort of pathological condition. However, recent studies seem to support the idea that this is a genuinely distinct species of human that lived as recently as 12,000 years ago.

A widely held theory holds that *H. floresiensis* is a diminutive offshoot of *H. erectus,* which is also known in the area. It has been suggested that the island's limited food supply resulted in the evolution of smaller humans.

As strange as these latest additions to the human story look, the discovery and analysis of *H. floresiensis* represents the continuing success of the basic methods used by paleoanthropologists and archaeologists—methods pioneered by the Leakeys and their colleagues. The same kinds of questions are asked each time a new fossil is found—for example:

- Does it represent the natural appearance of the species or might it have been distorted by geological forces or disease?
- What existing species does it most resemble? What are the anatomical similarities and differences?
- Can some differences be explained by a normal range of variations? (For example, what might a future scientist make of fossils of a huge NFL linebacker and a tiny ballet dancer?)

According to their inclination, experts may then push to lump the new find together with an existing species or split it off into a new species—or even a new genus.

NEW CHAPTER IN AN OLD CONTROVERSY

Louis and Mary Leakey's discoveries had led to a strong claim that *Homo habilis* was the immediate ancestor of humanity. The Leakeys placed the famous "handy Man" on the trunk of the human family tree, just below the branches that would become *Homo erectus* (and related species) and, eventually, modern *Homo sapiens*.

In 2011, however, researchers in South Africa led by Lee Berger of the University of Witwatersrand seemed to thrust the Leakeys' old nemesis *Australopithecus* back into the limelight. Just less than 2 million years ago, at least two members of that ancient genus, designated *Australopithecus sediba*, were buried in a deep cave and then entombed in a bed of sediment that preserved them in remarkably complete form.

Looking at the details of the fossilized hands and feet, Berger and his colleagues argued that they had features both of earlier apelike creatures (such as long, powerful fingers suited to gripping tree branches) and later human features (such as a thumb that could have enabled toolmaking). They have argued that *A. sediba*, not *H. habilis,* was the direct ancestor of *H. erectus.*

While not necessarily endorsing this linkage, Ian Tattersall agreed that the new findings would lead to a reexamination of the human family tree. Bernard Wood, another prominent expert, suggests that *A. sediba's* relatively

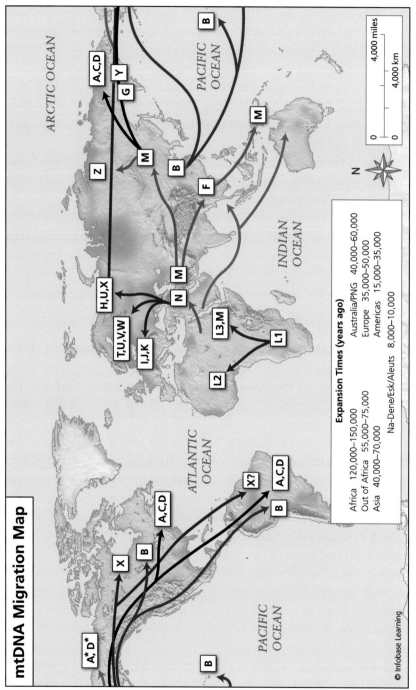

mtDNA Migration Map

A,C,D

Y

G

M

Z

B

F

M

H,U,X

T,U,V,W

I,J,K

N M

L3,M

L2

L1

B

ARCTIC OCEAN

PACIFIC OCEAN

INDIAN OCEAN

ATLANTIC OCEAN

PACIFIC OCEAN

A*,D*

X

B

A,C,D

X?

B A,C,D

B

N

Expansion Times (years ago)

Africa 120,000–150,000

Out of Africa 55,000–75,000

Asia 40,000–70,000

Australia/PNG 40,000–60,000

Europe 35,000–50,000

Americas 15,000–35,000

Na-Dene/Esk/Aleuts 8,000–10,000

0 ————— 4,000 miles

0 ————— 4,000 km

© Infobase Learning

Today, the study of the human genome offers another way to look at the migration of modern humans over the past 150,000 years—the letters refer to particular DNA sequences.

primitive brain would not have had time to evolve into the more capacious cranium of *H. erectus*. Instead, the mix of primitive and later human features in hands and feet may suggest that different parts of the anatomy evolve at different rates.

It seems that the possibilities for the human lineage keep getting more complicated. Just as in the Leakeys' day, the theoretical battle lines keep shifting as the painstaking quest for fossil evidence continues.

NEW TOOLS

Where there is legacy there is also change. During their careers, the Leakeys had to cope with the effects of new technology such as the potassium-argon dating that overthrew some of their cherished dates. Today, powerful techniques based on advances in genetics are revolutionizing many aspects of the study of prehistoric life.

The *molecular* (or genetic) *clock* is a method based on the observation that over time, organisms steadily accompany differences *(mutations)* in the arrangement of amino acids. Thus, if there is an evolutionary split of one species into two descendant species, the amount of change in the amino acids will be proportional to the length of time that has elapsed since the split. Dating by molecular clock is relative—to find out what a given difference means in years requires calibration, such as by analyzing fossils with known dates. Like earlier dating methods, the molecular clock has various limitations, and dating can be thrown off by the effects of changes in the rate and type of evolution, the effects of *natural selection,* or changes in the role played by the protein being analyzed.

A striking application of the molecular clock principle to *mitochondrial DNA (mtDNA)* was the determination that the common matrilineal ancestor of modern humans, the *Mitochondrial Eve,* lived in Africa about 200,000 years ago—news that surely would have pleased Louis Leakey! Using similar techniques, the split between the line leading to humans and that leading to chimpanzees has been estimated at about 6 million years ago.

In the finest tradition of the field, the new genetic and biochemical methods often conflict with the traditional analysis based on the anatomical features of the fossils. With all the change that may be coming to our understanding of human origins, one constant seems to be that bold scientists with firm beliefs in the correctness of their theories will continue the debate.

Chronology

August 7, 1903
Louis is born in British East Africa (now Kenya) to British missionaries May (Mary Bazett) and Harry Leakey

1904–1906
Due to Louis's father's illness, the family stays at Louis's grandmother's home in Reading, Berkshire, England

1907–1918
The Leakey family returns to Africa for most of this period. When he is older, Louis is allowed to live in a hut and learn the hunting and other skills of the Kikuyu natives. He also becomes fascinated with stone tools

February 6, 1913
Mary Douglas Nicol is born in London, England

1913
Hans Reck finds Olduvai Man

1919–1922
Louis attends Weymouth Secondary School in Boscombe, England, but has trouble adjusting to British ways

1922
Louis enters St. John's College, Cambridge, to study modern languages and prepare for a career as a missionary; his interest gradually shifts to anthropology and paleontology

1924–1925
Louis goes on his first expedition—a search for dinosaur fossils in Tanganyika; at the age of 12, Mary Nicol becomes fascinated by tools found in a French cave; the discovery of the Taung skull in South Africa *(Australopithecus africanus)* challenges the prevailing belief that Europe was the birthplace of humanity

1926

After graduating from Cambridge with honors in anthropology and archaeology, Louis organizes a field trip that explores Gamble's cave and other parts of Elmenteita

1927

Louis's first scientific paper, "Stone Age Man in Kenya Colony," is published in *Nature*

1928

Louis marries Henrietta Wilfrida (Frida) Avern

1929–1930

Louis's study of fossils at Cambridge leads him to push back the fossil human record to 600,000 years. His work is met with considerable skepticism; the first *Homo erectus* remains are found in China

1931–1932

Mary Nicol volunteers for archaeological digs and soon puts her artistic talent to work to illustrate the sites and the finds; Louis (with Hans Reck) makes his first trip to Olduvai Gorge; upon his return to England he meets Mary Nicol, and the two soon fall in love; Louis goes to Kanjera to look for fossils of the stone tool makers

1933

Louis's first book, *Adam's Ancestors,* is published; Louis and Frida have a son, Colin; The Royal Archaeological Institute gives qualified approval to Louis's finding of ancient human ancestors at Kanam and Kanjera; as a result of the extramarital affair with Mary, Cambridge panel investigates Louis for immorality, endangering his funding. However, Louis's mother provides funds for a new African expedition

1934

Louis returns to Kanam and Kanjera in an attempt to get more evidence, but the location of the site is lost

1935

Bitter recriminations in the battle over the dating of the Olduvai hominins lead to the final break between Louis and Cambridge

1936

Louis and Frida divorce; Louis marries Mary Nicol on December 24

1937
Louis and Mary receive a grant to study the Kikuyu in Kenya; Mary becomes gravely ill but recovers

1940
Louis and Mary have a son, Jonathan

1939–1944
World War II brings concerns about Italian, German, and (later) Japanese influence in Africa; Leakey is brought into the British Kenyan intelligence service and also does police and forensic work. Mary (and Louis, when time permits) continue archaeological excavations and work at the Coryndon Museum

1943
Louis and Mary uncover hundreds of stone tools at Olorgesailie

December 24, 1944
Louis and Mary have another son, Richard

1945
Louis gets a paid position as the curator of the Coryndon Museum, allowing him to resume fossil hunting

January 1947
Louis organizes and conducts a major conference, the first Pan-African Congress of Prehistory at Nairobi, Kenya. Leakey's scientific reputation is restored, and he is able to raise money for major expeditions

1948
Mary and Louis find the skull of *Proconsul africanus*

1949
Unrest in Kenya grows as settlers seek to strengthen white domination; Kikuyu form a secret society that becomes known as the Mau Mau; Louis and Mary have their third son, Philip

1950
Louis receives an honorary doctor of letters degree from Oxford University

1952
Kikuyu independence leader Jomo Kenyatta is arrested and sentenced to hard labor; Louis serves as court interpreter but is removed due to objections

1957
Louis hires Jane Morris Goodall as his secretary

1959

Mary discovers the skull of *Zinjanthropus boisei,* later renamed *Paranthropus boisei*

1960

The "Zinj" skull is dated to 1.75 million years ago, greatly pushing back the time line for human evolution; Louis finds the first African *Homo erectus* specimen; the National Geographic Society begins to sponsor the Leakey expeditions; Jane Goodall makes her first trip to Tanzania to study chimpanzees; at age 16, Richard leaves school and begins to support himself by trapping animals for photographers and scientists

1961

Louis resigns as curator of the Coryndon Museum and starts the Centre for Prehistory and Paleontology

1962

Louis and Mary receive the gold Hubbard Award, the highest honor awarded by the National Geographic Society; a hominid tooth is found and assigned the name *Homo habilis;* Richard starts a photo safari business, combining it with organizing fossil-hunting expeditions

1963

Kenya gains its independence. Its first president is Jomo Kenyattaa; Dian Fossey meets Louis while on safari in Africa; Louis helps organize excavations at Calico Hills in California's Mojave Desert. He argues that the human presence in the New World may date back 100,000 years or more (most authorities now accept a date of about 20,000 B.C.E.)

1964

Louis coauthors the article that introduces *Homo habilis* to the scientific world; Richard goes on his first expedition to Lake Natron, then goes to England to finish high school and study for a degree

1965

Richard marries Margaret Cropper, then returns to Kenya without going to college

1967

Richard leads the Kenyan part of an international expedition to the Omo Valley in Ethiopia. They find a 160,000-year-old fossil later identified as early *Homo sapiens;* Dian Fossey begins studying gorillas in Rwanda

1968

Richard leads his first expedition to Lake Turkana. He is also appointed administrative director of the Kenya National Museum; the L. S. B. Leakey Foundation for Research Related to Man's Origin is established; relations with Louis grow strained as Richard, aided by Kenyan allies, takes over the National Museum of Kenya; Richard is diagnosed with kidney disease

1969

Louis meets Birute Galdikas; Richard and Margaret separate; Richard is told his kidneys will fail within 10 years

1970

Louis organizes a controversial international paleontology conference at Calico Hills, California; Richard marries Meave Epps; Richard becomes director of the Kenya National Museum and makes extensive plans for its expansion

1971

Louis is the victim of a massive attack by bees; Birute and her husband begin Project Orangutan in Borneo

1972

In declining health, Louis Leakey dies in London from a heart attack; Richard and Bernard Ngeneo discover a *Homo habilis* skull (KNM-ER 1470) in Koobi Foora, Kenya; Richard and Meave's daughter Louise is born

1974

Donald Johanson discovers an early hominin skeleton in Ethiopia and names it Lucy

1975

Mary begins work at Laetoli

1976

Tim White's report reduces the date of Richard's Skull 1470 from 2.6 million to less than 2 million years ago; Mary discovers a trail of footprints left by upright-walking hominins about 3.6 million years ago

1978

Mary discovers a set of hominid footprints at Laetoli; Mary receives the Linnaeus Medal from the Swedish Royal Academy of Sciences but is upset by Donald Johanson's appropriation of her fossils

1979
Gravely ill, Richard receives a kidney transplant from his brother Philip; Richard's autobiography, *One Life*, is published

1981
Mary receives an honorary doctorate of letters degree from Oxford University; Richard and Donald Johanson engage in a sharp television debate over the structure of the human family tree

1982
Mary retires after losing part of her vision

1984
Richard and Kamoya Kimeu discover a nearly complete skeleton of a young *Homo erectus* that becomes known as Turkana Boy; Mary's autobiography *Disclosing the Past* is published

December 26, 1985
Dian Fossey is found murdered in her cabin at the Virunga gorilla study site

1989
Richard is appointed the head of the Kenyan Wildlife Conservation and Management Department. He begins a vigorous war against wildlife poachers, particularly with regard to the illicit ivory trade

1993
Richard loses the lower portions of both legs when his small plane crashes; Louise Leakey takes charge of the Lake Turkana expeditions

1994
Richard resigns from the Kenya Wildlife Service amid charges of corruption and mismanagement against some officials

1995
Richard enters politics, joining Kenyan reformers in launching the Safina Party. The dominant KANU party of Daniel arap Moi largely suppresses and marginalizes the reform movement

December 9, 1996
Mary Leakey dies in Nairobi, Kenya

1999–2001
Richard is appointed head of the Kenyan Civil Service at the insistence of foreign aid donors

2001

Meave and Louise Leakey announce the discovery of *Kenyanthropos platyops,* an early hominin whose place in the family tree remains controversial

2002

Richard serves as a professor of anthropology at Stony Brook University in New York

2004

Richard establishes WildlifeDirect, a charity designed to support Kenyan conservationists and help them establish online links to international supporters

2007

Richard heads the Kenyan branch of Transparency International

September 2011

The discovery of well-preserved fossils of *Australopithecus sediba* raises new questions about the ancestry of archaic and modern humans

Glossary

absolute dating   a means of dating (such as measuring radioactive decay) that does not depend on the geological location or relative position of the fossil or other material.

Acheulian   a time in the early Stone Age (from roughly 1.5 million to 200,000 years ago) when early humans made stone tools, such as bifacial (two sided) hand axes.

anthropology   the study of human beings, including their physical remains, artifacts (archaeology), and culture.

ape   nonhuman primates such as the chimpanzee, gorilla, and orangutan (but not monkeys).

archaeology   the study of ancient cultures and behavior through the artifacts and other traces they leave behind.

artifact   an object made or modified by humans, such as a tool.

australopithecines   A genus of extinct bipedal hominid primates. It is uncertain whether they are direct ancestors on the human line.

Australopithecus afarensis   A species of gracile (light-bodied) australopithecine that lived about 3.5 million years ago. The most famous example is Lucy.

Australopithecus boisei   A robust australopithecine species discovered by the Leakeys in East Africa, originally named *Zinjanthropus boisei* and also known today as *Paranthropus boisei*.

bipedal   able to walk upright on two legs.

Chellean   see OLDOWAN.

common ancestor   the earliest ancestor shared by two or more species or other taxa.

cranium   a skull without the mandible.

culture   the totality of human behavior and expression, including technology, myth and religion, arts, and so on.

DNA (deoxyribonucleic acid)   the large, complex organic molecule whose arrangement specifies the genetic code for the synthesis of proteins and ultimately the physical structure of organisms.

evolution   change in a population over time, including genetic change and the emergence of new species.

flint   a form of quartz that often comes in lumps (nodules) and can be used to make stone tools.

fossil   the preserved remains or traces of animals or plants from the remote past.

genetic distance   a measure of how much the genes differ between two groups or lineages.

genus   the next higher classification above species; for example, the genus *Homo* includes species such as *habilis* and *erectus*.

geochronology   relative dating of fossils based on geological processes, such as changes in sea level.

geology   the study of rocks, soil, and other features of the Earth's crust.

gracile   relatively light and delicate in body form.

holotype   the fossil of a particular species that becomes the standard against which others are compared.

hominin   (formerly hominid) a broad term for humans and those species related to them.

Homo   the genus that includes modern humans and their extinct relatives.

Homo erectus   an early form of human with a larger brain than *Homo habilis*. *Homo erectus* lived between 1.8 million and 300,000 years ago and spread from Africa widely into Europe and Asia.

Homo habilis   the earliest known species in genus *Homo*. While still primitive, it had a larger brain and more human characteristics than the earlier australopithecines.

Homo sapiens   literally "wise man," is the species name for modern humanity, originating in Africa perhaps 200,000 years ago.

horizon   in archaeology, a distinct cultural period as displayed in remains and artifacts.

hypothesis   a scientific idea or assertion that can be proven or disproved through observation or experiment.

in situ   a fossil or artifact that is in the place it was originally deposited.

lineage   a group of species descended from a common ancestor.

Lucy   the first *Australopithecus afarensis* specimen discovered by Donald Johanson in 1974.

lumpers   researchers who tend to place a higher value on similarities than differences among specimens and thus resist declaring new species.

mandible   the lower jaw.

Miocene   a geological period from about 23 million years ago to about 5.3 million years ago.

missing link   an intermediate form between ape and human that was sought in the 19th and early 20th centuries. Today, the picture of human descent is more complex, with multiple links possible.

mitochondrial DNA (mtDNA)   genetic material in mitochondria (bodies that process chemicals within cells) that is passed on only through the mother.

mitochondrial Eve   the last common ancestor of modern humans, dated through changes in mtDNA. This ancestor (who is not an individual woman) is believed to have lived about 200,000 years ago.

modern humans   the first members of our species *(Homo sapiens)* who had essentially the same physical characteristics as people today, although they did not necessarily have the same behavioral or mental capacities.

molecular clock   a technique for determining when two species or lineages diverged, based on the rate of mutation or change in molecular sequences (usually in DNA or proteins).

multiregional hypothesis   the hypothesis that after the earliest humans spread from Africa, they evolved separately into modern forms.

mutation   a change in a genetic sequence.

natural selection   the process by which those traits that allow for better survival of offspring become dominant in a population of organisms.

Neolithic   New Stone Age, the period starting around 12,000 years ago and characterized by the development of agriculture, and ending with the widespread use of metal.

obsidian   a glasslike mineral (often black and shiny) that can be used to make sharp tools.

Oldowan   the earliest form of stone tools, consisting of choppers and flakes and produced by hammering one stone with another. These techniques began about 2.5 million years ago.

Out-of-Africa hypothesis   the hypothesis that modern humans represent the last of a series of waves of migration of humans from Africa.

paleoanthropology   the study of early humans and related species by examining the fossils or other traces they left behind.

Paleolithic   the Old Stone Age, beginning with the first stone tools about 2.5 million years ago and ending with development of agriculture in the Neolithic about 12,000 years ago.

paleontology   the study of extinct organisms, usually by examining fossils.

Pleisotocene   the geological time period from about 1.8 million to 10,000 years ago. In archaeological terms it roughly corresponds to the Paleolithic, or Old Stone Age.

Pliocene   the geological time period from about 5 million to 1.8 million years ago. Australopithecines and early humans developed during this period.

primate   a family of mammals that includes humans, apes, and monkeys.

Proconsul   an early primate, considered to be a common ancestor of both apes and monkeys.

radiometric dating   any technique for dating that is based on processes such as radioactive decay or the effects of radioactivity on surrounding material. Each method is applicable only to a certain range of time. Examples include carbon (carbon-14) dating and potassium-argon dating.

relative date   a date that is not absolute but only earlier or later than that of some other event, such as one layer of sediment being laid down after another.

robust   having a heavily built body. For australopithecines this refers particularly to large molars, thick jaws, and powerful muscles for chewing.

sagittal crest   an arched bone protruding from the top of the skull.

species   a population of organisms that can interbreed to produce fertile offspring. Species can also be defined in morphological (body structure), genetic, or ecological terms.

splitters   researchers who emphasize the observed differences between specimens, thus tending to identify them as belonging to separate species.

theory   a comprehensive scientific explanation that can be used to make predictions. Theories such as evolution have been well tested through numerous observations.

tool   an object that can be used for a particular purpose. In paleoanthropology the term is usually restricted to an object that has been fashioned or modified in some way, such as a stone core or flake.

tuff   volcanic ash that is deposited in layers.

Further Resources

Books

Cole, Sonia Mary. *Leakey's Luck: The Life of Louis Seymour Bazett Leakey, 1903–1972.* New York: Harcourt, 1975.

An older biography, but contains many interesting details about Leakey's life and work.

Darwin, Charles. *The Illustrated Origin of Species.* New York: Hill & Wang, 1979.

An accessible edition of Darwin's classic work on evolution.

Gibbons, Ann. *The First Human: The Race to Discover Our Earliest Ancestors.* New York: Doubleday, 2006.

An account of today's field research, where physical challenges, tricky scientific issues, and politics (both African and professional) must be faced in the struggle to unearth and explain human ancestors.

Hellman, Hal. *Great Feuds in Science: Ten of the Liveliest Disputes Ever.* New York: Wiley, 1999.

Includes a chapter on the dispute between Donald Johanson and the Leakeys over the proper arrangement of the human family tree.

Johanson, Donald, and Kate Wong. *Lucy's Legacy: The Quest for Human Origins.* New York: Three Rivers Press, 2010.

Johanson's latest work combines an engaging look at the day-to-day work in the field (tedious and frustrating as well as exciting) with an appraisal of the latest controversies, including the relation between modern humans and Neanderthals and the discovery of diminutive hobbit hominins in Indonesia.

———, and Maitland Edey. *Lucy: The Beginnings of Humankind.* New York: Warner, 1982.

The classic (and still valuable) account of the discovery of Lucy, one of the most important human ancestors.

Kalb, Jon. *Adventures in the Bone Trade: The Race to Discover Human Ancestors in Ethiopia's Afar Depression.* New York: Copernicus, 2001.
   A geologist who mapped the Afar region in Ethiopia recounts the treacherous climate, fierce competition between fossil hunters, political upheaval, and even war that has marked this crucible of early humanity.

Kruhm, Mary Bowman. *The Leakeys: A Biography.* Amherst, N.Y.: Prometheus Books, 2010.
   A recent biography with a good mix of anecdote and scientific background. It continues the story into the third generation (Louise Leakey, daughter of Richard and Meave).

Leakey, Louis Seymour Bazett. *By the Evidence: Memoirs, 1932–1951.* New York: Harcourt, 1976.
   The second volume of Louis Leakey's autobiography. Engaging and opinionated like the man himself.

———. *White African.* Cambridge, Mass.: Schenkman, 1966.
   The first volume of Louis Leakey's autobiography. Features his childhood in Africa.

Leakey, Mary. *Disclosing the Past.* New York: Doubleday, 1984.
   Mary Leakey's autobiography, which includes much that she had not spoken about publicly before.

Leakey, Richard. *One Life.* Salem, N.H.: Salem House, 1984.
   Richard Leakey's autobiography, covering his career up to the Lake Turkana excavations, but not his later work in protecting wildlife.

———, and Roger Lewin. *Origins Reconsidered: In Search of What Make Us Human.* New York: Anchor, 1993.
   Richard Leakey's summary of developments in the study of human origins and reflections on his work and its significance.

———, and Virginia Morrell. *Wildlife Wars: My Fight to Save Africa's Natural Treasures.* New York: St. Martins, 2001.
   A harrowing and often impassioned account of Richard Leakey's struggle to stop the destruction of elephants and other wildlife in Kenya and other parts of Africa.

Lewin, Roger. *Bones of Contention: Controversies in the Search for Human Origins.* Chicago: University of Chicago Press, 1997.

Rather than the discoveries, the author focuses on how they are inter-preted—with biases and preconceptions coming into play at every turn. A classic example is the early portrayals of the Neanderthals as primitive brutes. The story continues to the battles between Donald Johanson and the Leakeys in more recent times.

———. *Human Evolution: An Illustrated Introduction.* 5th ed. Malden, Mass.: Blackwell, 2005.
A textbook-like presentation, but clear and well-organized in presenting the current knowledge in the field and the techniques used by researchers.

Morrell, Virginia. *Ancestral Passions: The Leakey Family and the Quest for Humankind's Beginnings.* New York: Touchstone, 1996.
A compelling biography of the "first family" of paleontology, in which Louis Leakey, joined by second wife Mary and their son Richard, struggled to defend their work against newer rivals even as father and son clashed over its future direction.

Robertshaw, Peter, ed. *A History of African Archaeology.* Portsmouth, N.H.: Heinemann, 1990.
An account of nearly two centuries of archeological research in Africa, describing how expeditions were organized and carried out.

Stanford, Craig. *Upright: The Evolutionary Key to Becoming Human.* Boston, Mass.: Houghton Mifflin, 2003.
What was the key to accelerating hominid evolution-bigger brains or upright posture? The author argues that the ability to walk on two legs (freeing the hands for other uses) led to a cascade of changes in behavior and eventually, anatomy.

Tattersall, Ian. *The Fossil Trail: How We Know What We Think We Know About Human Evolution.* 2nd edition. New York: Oxford University Press, 2008.
Far from a dry catalog of fossils, this account weaves together fossil discoveries and conflicting interpretations to draw a possible evolutionary tree of humans. The variety of human-like species is explained by adaptation to shifts in climate and the challenges of different environments.

———. *The Monkey in the Mirror: Essays on the Science of What Makes Us Human.* New York: Mariner Books, 2003.
Eight engaging essays that look at the nature of the scientific process, "themes" of developing humanity (such as upright walking and tool use), mysteries surrounding the Neanderthals, and the emergence of modern humanity.

Willis, Delta. *The Hominid Gang: Behind the Scenes in the Search for Human Origins.* New York: Penguin, 1991.

The author's encounters in the field with leading paleontologists, probing how they work, the key issues in understanding human origins, and the many controversies that have arisen between leading researchers such as the Leakeys and Donald Johanson.

Periodicals

Bellows, Keith. "Pursuing Our Past in Africa: A Paleoanthropologist Carries on the Work of Her Parents and Grandparents." *National Geographic Traveler* (September 2008).

Louise Leakey talks about her grandparents and parents as well as her own work in studying African prehistory and helping today's Africans.

Leakey, Richard, and Alan Walker. "*Homo erectus* Unearthed." *National Geographic* 168, no. 5 (November 1985): pp. 625–629.

An account of the discovery and analysis of Turkana Boy.

Payne, Melvin M. "Family in Search of Prehistoric Man." *National Geographic* (February 1965): p. 200 ff.

A contemporary account of the activities of Louis and Mary Leakey in Olduvai.

———. "The Leakey Tradition Lives On." *National Geographic* 143, no. 1 (January 1973): pp. 143–144.

An assessment of the Leakey legacy following the death of Louis.

Wade, Nicholas. "New Fossils May Redraw Human Family Tree." *New York Times*, September 8, 2011. Also available online. URL: http://www.nytimes.com/2011/09/09/science/09fossils.html?_r=2&hp. Accessed September 12, 2011.

Recent findings of Australopithecus sediba *fossils with a mixture of ape-like and humanlike characteristics may displace* Homo habilis *as the direct ancestor of archaic and modern humans. However, a variety of other interpretations is possible.*

Internet Resources

"Archaeology Fieldwork." Discovery.com. Available online. URL: http://curiosity.discovery.com/topic/archaeology-fieldwork. Accessed March 28, 2011.

Answers a variety of questions about what archaeologists do in the field, their tools, and techniques.

Hernandez, Christina. SmartPlanet, May 13, 2010. "Louise Leakey on What Ancient Fossils Tell Us about Our Future." Available online. URL: http://www.smartplanet.com/people/blog/pure-genius/louise-leakey-on-what-ancient-fossils-tell-us-about-our-future/3663/. Accessed March 28, 2011.

Louise Leakey carries on the family tradition, extending it into comprehensive research projects at Lake Turkana and Koobi Fora.

Hunter-Gault, Charlayne. "Mary Leakey, Fossil Hunter." PBS Online Newshour, December 9, 1996. Available online. URL: http://www.pbs.org/newshour/bb/remember/leakey_12-9.html. Accessed March 28, 2011.

An interview with Smithsonian scholar Richard Potts about Mary Leakey's life and legacy.

The Leakey Foundation. Available online. URL: http://leakeyfoundation.org/. Accessed March 28, 2011.

An educational and research foundation, part of the Leakey legacy. The site includes news and resources.

"Louise Leakey Digs for Humanity's Origins." TED: Ideas Worth Spreading. February 2008. Available online. URL: http://www.ted.com/talks/louise_leakey_digs_for_humanity_s_origins.html. Accessed August 8, 2011.

Louise Leakey talks about her work, giving a survey of what is known about human origins and arguing that humans and other primates "have a common past and a common future."

National Museums of Kenya Web site. Available online. URL: http://www.museums.or.ke. Accessed March 28, 2011.

An opportunity to explore the institution to which the Leakeys contributed so much.

Suarez, Ray. "New Beginnings." PBS Online Newshour, March 26, 2001. Available online. URL: http://www.pbs.org/newshour/bb/science/jan-june01/newbegin_03-26.html. Accessed March 28, 2011.

PBS commentator Ray Suarez interviews Meave Leakey about her 1999 discovery of a 3.5 million year old human skull.

"A Timeline of Fossil Discoveries." Australian Museum. Available online. URL: http://australianmuseum.net.au/A-timeline-of-fossil-discoveries. Accessed March 28, 2011.

A useful summary of the major human fossil finds, organized by decade and year, with many illustrations of specimens.

Index

at Hyrax Hill, 40
obsidian, 6–8, 15
at Olduvai, 21–22, 23, 25, 28, 60
at Olorgesailie, 43
rocks as, 7
Transparency International, 100
Turkana, Lake. *See* Rudolf, Lake
Turkana Basin Institute, 100
Turkana Boy, 70, 96–98, 97*f*

V

Van Riet Lowe, Clarence, 31
Victoria, Lake, 35, 45
Virunga National Park, 79–80, 100

W

Wahu, Grace, 59
Walker, Alan, 97, 98
Waterfall Cave, 39
Wenner-Gren Foundation, 31
Western, David, 92

Weymouth Secondary School, 8–9
White, Tim, 90, 94
White African (L. Leakey)
    on Cambridge University, 13, 14
    on childhood, 2, 3, 6
    on Gamble caves, 19
    on Olduvai, 21–22, 23
    publication of, 38
    on secondary school, 8–9
Whitworth, Thomas, 57
Wildlife Direct, 100
Wildlife Service (Kenya), 99
Wood, Bernard, 103–105
World War I, 5
World War II, 41–42

Z

"Zinj," 61–66, 61*f*, 63*f*, 65*f*, 66*f*
Zinjanthropus boisei. See Paranthropus boisei
Zoological Society of London, 87